A Study Guide and Map Supplement

for

The Western Experience

Volume I
To The Eighteenth Century

Seventh Edition

A Study Guide and Map Supplement

for

The Western Experience

Volume I
To The Eighteenth Century

Seventh Edition

Mortimer Chambers

University of California, Los Angeles

Raymond Grew

University of Michigan

Barbara Hanawalt

University of Minnesota

Theodore K. Rabb

Princeton University

Isser Woloch

Columbia University

Prepared by

Edward W. M. Bever

State University of New York College at Old Westbury

McGraw-Hill College

Boston   Burr Ridge, IL   Dubuque, IA   Madison, WI   New York   San Francisco   St. Louis
Bangkok   Bogotá   Caracas   Lisbon   London   Madrid
Mexico City   Milan   New Delhi   Seoul   Singapore   Sydney   Taipei   Toronto

McGraw-Hill College

A Division of The McGraw-Hill Companies

A Study Guide and Map Supplement for use with
THE WESTERN EXPERIENCE, VOLUME I: TO THE EIGHTEENTH CENTURY

1 2 3 4 5 6 7 8 9 0 EBI/EBI 9 0 9 8

ISBN 0-07-012955-X

www.mhhe.com

Dennis Sherman is Professor of History at John Jay College of Criminal Justice, the City University of New York. He received his B.A. (1962) and J.D. (1965) from the University of California at Berkeley and his Ph.D. (1970) from the University of Michigan. He was Visiting Professor at the University of Paris (1978–1979; 1985). He received the Ford Foundation Prize Fellowship (1968–1969, 1969–1970), a fellowship from the Council for Research on Economic History (1971–1972), and fellowships from the National Endowment for the Humanities (1973–1976). His publications include *A Short History of Western Civilization*, Eighth Edition, 1994 (co-author), *Western Civilization: Sources, Images, and Interpretations*, Fourth Edition, 1995, *World Civilizations: Sources, Images, and Interpretations*, 1994 (co-author), a series of introductions in the Garland Library of War and Peace, several articles and reviews on nineteenth-century French economic and social history in American and European journals, and short fiction in literary journals.

Edward Bever is Assistant Professor of History at the State University of New York College at Old Westbury. He received his B.A. (1975) from Dartmouth College and his M.A. (1978) and Ph.D. (1983) from Princeton University. From 1984 to 1997 he worked as a software developer specializing in historical simulations and reference works. During this time he taught a variety of courses in European and African history and Western Civilization at Drew University, Purchase College, Loyola College of Maryland, Monmouth College, and Mercer County College in New Jersey. His software creations include *Crusade in Europe* (1985), *Conflict in Vietnam* (1986), *Revolution '76* (1989) and *No Greater Glory* (1991), and he wrote a series of essays and designed a set of maps surveying Western Civilization for the multimedia reference work *Culture 2.0* (1991). His written publications include a book on African political history, *Africa* (1996); extensive historical background material to accompany his software; and scholarly articles, reviews, and papers on popular culture and witchcraft trials in early modern Europe.

CONTENTS

PREFACE

This new edition of the *Study Guide* reflects the changes in the Seventh Edition of *The Western Experience,* in particular the substantial revisions that have been made to the Medieval chapters. Each chapter in the Seventh Edition, reflects a decision to significantly recast the presentation of material in the *Guide* itself in order to make it more interactive and more self contained.

To those ends, the chapter summaries have been replaced by sets of multiple choice self test questions; some of the questions in the Guide to the Documents sections have been made into multiple choice questions; and the Significant Individuals and Identification sections have been transformed into matching exercises. The effect of the new formats is to make using the *Guide* more active, while the inclusion of answers at the end of each chapter makes it possible to get immediate feedback about how well material is being understood. The Chapter Highlights, Chapter Outline, and Transitions sections still summarize the main points of the chapters, and the Problems for Analysis, Speculations, and some of the Guide to the Documents questions are presented in the open-ended, "essay question" style that is generally stressed in college courses, so the overall effect of the changes has been to add new approaches to the material without losing the value of the old.

Two final changes to the *Study Guide* have been made in the section summaries. One is the addition of a Cultural Styles section, which poses questions about works of art from different civilizations and eras. The purpose of this section is to highlight the visual information contained in the textbook's rich set of illustrations about the characteristics of, links between, and differences among the periods and traditions in Western Civilization.

The other change to the section summaries is a recasting of the Box Charts. They now provide a framework in which to organize the material according to the overarching themes identified by the authors in the introduction to the textbook. The intent of this change is to move focus away from the particularities of the different eras to the underlying structures of human existence that inform the authors' presentation. In this way, the long-term development of Western Civilization can be followed within a standard frame of reference that is implicit in the main text. Using these standard categories to organize the material should help bring order and meaning to the immense and complex story of *The Western Experience*.

WHAT IS HISTORY?

Definition

History is the record of the human past. It includes both the more concrete elements of the past such as our wars, governments, and creations, and the more elusive ones such as hopes, fantasies, and failures over time. Historians study this human past in order to discover what people thought and did, and then they organize these findings into a broad chronological framework. To do this, they look at the records humans have left of their past, the most important of which are written. Although nonwritten records, such as artifacts, buildings, oral traditions, and paintings, are also sources for the study of the human past, the period before written records appear is usually considered "pre-history."

The Purposes of History

History can be used for various purposes. First, a systematic study of the past helps us to understand human nature; in short, history can be used to give us an idea of who we are as human beings. Second, it can be used to gain insights into contemporary affairs, either through a study of the developments that have shaped the present or through the use of analogies to related circumstances of the past. Third, societies use history to socialize the young, that is, to teach them how to behave and think in culturally and socially appropriate ways.

Orientation

Historians approach the study of history from two main perspectives: the humanities and the social sciences. Those with a humanities orientation see history as being made up of unique people, actions, and events, which are to be studied both for their intrinsic value and for the insights they provide about humans in a particular set of historical circumstances. Those with a social science orientation look for patterns in human thought and behavior over time. They focus on comparisons rather than on unique events and are more willing to draw conclusions related to present problems. The authors of *The Western Experience*, Seventh Edition, use both perspectives.

Styles

In writing history, historians traditionally use two main styles: narrative and analytic. Those who prefer the narrative style emphasize a chronological sequence of events. Their histories are more like stories, describing the events from the beginning to the end. Historians who prefer the analytic style emphasize explanation. Their histories deal more with topics, focusing on causes and relationships. Most historians use both styles but show a definite preference for one or the other. The authors of *The Western Experience* stress the analytic style.

Interpretations

Some historians have a particular interpretation or philosophy of history, that is, a way of understanding its meaning and of interpreting its most important aspects. Marxist historians, for example, argue that economic forces are most important, influencing politics, culture, and society in profound ways. They view history organically, following a path in relatively predictable ways. Their interpretations are occasionally pointed out in *The Western Experience*. Most historians are not committed to a particular philosophy of history, but they do interpret major historical developments in certain ways. Thus, for example, there are various groups of historians who emphasize a social interpretation of the French Revolution of 1789, while there are others who argue that the Revolution is best understood in political and economic terms. The authors of *The Western Experience* are relatively eclectic; they use a variety of interpretations and often indicate major points of interpretive disagreement among historians.

Common Concerns

The style, orientation, and philosophy of most modern historians are not at one extreme or the other. Moreover, the concerns they share outweigh their differences. All historians want to know what happened, when it happened, and how it happened. While the question of cause is touchy, historians all want to know why something happened, and they are all particularly interested in studying change over time.

THE HISTORICAL METHOD

Process

1. *Search for Sources:* One of the first tasks a historian faces is the search for sources. Most sources are written documents, which include everything from gravestone inscriptions and diaries to books and governmental records. Other sources include buildings, art, maps, pottery, and oral traditions. In searching for sources, historians do not work at random. They usually have something in mind before they start, and in the process, they must decide which sources to emphasize over others.

2. *External Criticism:* To test the genuineness of the source, historians must engage in external criticism. This constitutes an attempt to uncover forgeries and errors. Some startling revisions of history have resulted from effective criticism of previously accepted sources.

3. *Internal Criticism:* A source, though genuine, may not be objective, or it may reveal something that was not apparent at first. To deal with this, historians subject sources to internal criticism by such methods as evaluating the motives of the person who wrote the document, looking for inconsistencies within the source, and comparing different meanings of a word or phrase used in the source.

4. *Synthesis:* Finally, the historian creates a synthesis. He or she gathers the relevant sources together, applies them to the question being investigated, decides what is to be included, and writes a history. This oversimplifies the process, for historians often search, criticize, and synthesize at the same time. Moreover, the process is not as objective as it seems, for historians select what they think is most important and what fits into their own philosophy or interpretation of history.

Categories

Historians use certain categories to organize different types of information. The number and boundaries of these differ according to what each historian thinks is most useful. The principal categories are as follows:

1. *Political:* This refers to questions of how humans are governed, including such matters as the exercise of power in peace and war, the use of law, the formation of governments, the collection of taxes, and the establishment of public services.

2. *Economic:* This refers to the production and distribution of goods and services. On the production side, historians usually focus on agriculture, commerce, manufacturing, and finance. On the distribution side, they deal with who gets how much of what is produced. Their problem is supply and demand and how people earn their living.

3. *Social:* This is the broadest category. It refers to relations between individuals or groups within some sort of community. This includes the institutions people create (the family, the army), the classes or castes to which people belong (the working class, the aristocracy), the customs people follow (marriage, eating), the activities people engage in together (sports, drinking), and the attitudes people share (toward foreigners, commerce).

4. *Intellectual:* This refers to the ideas, theories, and beliefs expressed by people in some organized way about topics thought to be important. This includes such matters as political theories, scientific ideas, and philosophies of life.

5. *Religious:* This refers to theories, beliefs, and practices related to the supernatural or the unknown. This includes such matters as the growth of religious institutions, the formation of beliefs about the relation between human beings and God, and the practice of rituals and festivals.

6. *Cultural:* This refers to the ideas, values, and expressions of human beings as evidenced in aesthetic works, such as music, art, and literature.

While most historians work with these categories on a relatively *ad hoc* basis, some attempt to define them in a way that provides a comprehensive structure to history and human experience. The authors of *The Western Experience* discuss in the introduction to the textbook the categories that they see as structuring human affairs: Social Structures (Groups in Society), Political Events and Structures, the Economics of Production and Distribution, Family (including Gender Roles and Daily Life), War, Religion, and Cultural Expression (including intellectual life). While they do not use these categories explicitly to structure the book, they incorporate them implicitly throughout it.

In addition to organizing different types of information into categories, historians often specialize in one or two of these. For example, some historians focus on political history, whereas others are concerned with social-economic history. The best historians bring to bear on the problems that interest them, however specialized the problems may seem, data from all these categories.

DOCUMENTS

Historians classify written documents into two types: primary and secondary. Primary documents are those written by a person living during the period being studied and participating in the matter under investigation. A primary document is looked at as a piece of evidence that shows what people thought, how they acted, and what they accomplished. A secondary document is usually written by someone after the period of time that is being studied. It is either mainly a description or an interpretation of the topic being studied: the more descriptive it is, the more it simply traces what happened; the more interpretive it is, the more it analyzes the causes or the significance of what happened.

PERIODIZATION

Historians cannot deal with all of history at once. One way to solve this is to break history up into separate periods. How this is done is a matter of discretion; what is important is the division of a time into periods that can be dealt with as a whole, without doing too much violence to the continuity of history. Typically, Western Civilization is divided into the Ancient World, the Middle Ages, the Renaissance and Reformation, the Early Modern World, the nineteenth century (1789–1914), and the twentieth century (1914–present), as illustrated by the section summaries in this study guide. There are a number of subdivisions that can be made within these periods. *The Western Experience* is divided into both periodic and topical chapters.

STUDY AIDS

Reading

There is no way to get around reading—the more you read, the better you become at it. Thus the best advice is to read the assigned chapters. But there are some techniques that will make the task easier. First, think about the title of the book you are reading; often, it tells much about what is in the book. Second, read through the chapter headings and subheadings. Whatever you read will make more sense and will be more easily remembered if it is placed in the context of the section, the chapter, and the book as a whole. Third, concentrate on the first and last paragraphs or two of each chapter and each major section of the chapter. Often, the author will summarize in these areas what he or she wants to communicate. Finally, concentrate on the first sentence of each paragraph. Often, but not always, the first sentence is a topic sentence, making the point for which the rest of the paragraph is an expansion.

Underlining (or Highlighting) and Writing in the Margins

The easiest and quickest way to begin mastering the material in the book is to underline or highlight important points and ideas as you go along. An underlined or highlighted passage can be surveyed and reviewed much more quickly than a clear one, whether the purpose is to take notes (see below), to find material for an essay, or to review for a test. Comments in the margins can also be useful; they can be made to summarize long passages, to call out key terms, or to remind yourself about your reactions to the author's points.

Some students are reluctant to mark in books, either out of a misguided reverence for printed material or out of an equally misguided desire to resell the text back to the bookstore at the end of the course. The latter concern is simply short-sighted, for considering the cost of a college course, the cost of the textbook is minor, and avoiding techniques that will help wring the full value from the major investment to recoup the minor one is being penny wise and pound foolish. The former concern, a reverential attitude towards printed materials, is a vestige from long ago, when books were rare and precious things. They are still precious, but they are not rare, and there's nothing wrong with a well-used textbook looking well-used. You own the book; make it your own.

Note that this approach should NOT be taken to library books. Other people need to use them for their own purposes, so personalizing them in this way is inconsiderate.

Note Taking

1. *Reading Assignments:* While it is easier said than done, it is of tremendous advantage to take notes on reading assignments. Taking notes, if done properly, will help you to integrate the readings into your mind much more than simply reading them. Moreover, notes will ease the problem of review for papers, exams, or classroom discussions.

There are a number of ways to take notes. Generally, you should use an outline form, following the main points or headings of each chapter. Under each section of your outline you should include the important points and information, translated into your own words. After each section of a chapter ask yourself, "What is the author trying to say here, what is the author trying to convey?" It may be easier to copy phrases or words used by the author, but it is much more effective if you can transform them into your own words. While facts, names, and dates are important, avoid simply making a list of them without focusing on the more general interpretation, development, or topic that the author is discussing. Indicate the kinds of evidence the author uses, what the author's interpretations are, and to what degree you agree with what he or she says (does it make sense to you?). Some students prefer to underline in the text and write notes in the margins. This is a less time-consuming, easier, and often useful method, but probably not as effective as outlining and using your own words to summarize each section. As with many things, it is the extra effort involved that leads to the more effective learning.

2. *Lectures and Classes:* Much of what has been said also applies to taking notes in class. The trick is to write just enough to get the main points without losing track of what is going on in class. Concentrate on the major points the speaker is trying to make, not simply all the facts. Do not try to write down everything or to write in complete sentences; try to develop a method of writing down key words or phrases that works for you. The most important thing is the act of taking notes, for taking notes involves you actively with the class material. Not taking notes, in contrast, leads to a passive state of listening, and soon, daydreaming, at which point much of what is said will go in one ear and out the other.

A couple of additional tips might help. First, be ready at the beginning of class. Often, the point of a whole lecture or discussion is outlined in the first couple of minutes; missing it makes much of what you hear seem out of context. Second, go over your notes after class. A few minutes spent reviewing the main points while they are fresh in your mind can make studying the material later much easier.

Writing

There are three steps that you should take before writing a paper. First, carefully read the question or topic you are to write on; at times, good papers are written on the wrong topic. If you are to make up a topic, spend some time on it. Think of your topic as a question. It should not be unanswerably broad (what is the history of Western Civilization?) or insignificantly narrow (when was toothpaste invented?). It will be something that interests you and that is easily researched. Second, start reading about the topic, taking notes on the main points. Third, after some reading, start writing an outline of the main points you want to make. Revise this outline a number of times, arranging your points in some logical way and making sure all your points help answer the question or support the argument you are making.

A paper should have three parts: an introduction, a body, and a conclusion. For a short paper, your introduction should be only a paragraph or two in length; for a long paper, perhaps one or two pages. In the introduction tell the reader what the general topic is, what you will argue about the topic, and why it is important or interesting. This is an extremely important part of a paper, often neglected by students. You can win or lose the reader with the introduction. You may find it easier to leave the introduction until after you have written the body of the paper, especially if it is difficult to get started writing. In the body, make your argument. Generally, make one major point in each paragraph, usually in the first sentence (topic sentence). The rest of the paragraph should contain explanation, expansion, support, illustration, or evidence for this point. In the paragraph, you should make it clear how this point helps answer the question. Your paragraphs should be organized in some logical order (chronological, from strongest to weakest point, categories). Finally, in the conclusion, tell the reader—in different words—what you have argued in the body of the paper, and indicate why what you have argued is important. The conclusion, like the introduction, is a particularly important and yet an often slighted part of a paper.

Most of the same suggestions for papers apply to essay exams. Even more emphasis should be placed on making sure you know what the question asks. Spend some time outlining your answer. As with papers, you should have an introduction, body, and conclusion, even if they are all relatively short. For each point you make, try to supply some evidence as support. Keep to the indicated time limits.

Class Participation

Class participation is difficult for many students, yet there is no better way to get over this difficulty than to do it. Try and force yourself to ask questions or indicate your point of view when appropriate times arise. If this is particularly difficult for you, it may help to talk about it with other students or with the teacher privately.

Studying

If you have a style of studying that works well for you, stick to it. If not, try to do three things: keep up with all your assignments regularly, work with someone else, and spend some extra time reviewing before exams.

HOW TO USE THIS GUIDE

There is one chapter in this guide corresponding to each chapter in *The Western Experience*. Each chapter of the guide is divided into a number of sections.

   1. *Chapter Highlights:* The main points of each chapter are introduced here. Part of the purpose in doing this is to emphasize the importance of not losing sight of the broader concerns of the chapter as you study its specific sections. By returning to these main themes and expanding upon them after you read the chapter, they can become a tool to help you grasp more firmly what the chapter is about.

   2. *Chapter Outline:* Here, the chapter is outlined using the major headings in the text. The purpose is to provide an overview of the chapter so that what you read will make more sense and will be more easily remembered because it can be seen in the context of the section, the chapter, and the book as a whole.

   3. *Self Test:* This section contains approximately 20 multiple choice questions. In general, there are one or two questions per sub-heading, and they are presented in the order of the sections in the text. The purpose of these questions is to help focus your reading of the text. Note that they are not written as mock-test questions, but instead are styled to help you master the material. Thus, there are many questions that ask which one of the four possibilities is NOT correct, so that you will spend more time thinking about the correct information than about wrong answers. Many of the questions have been written to emphasize the broad concepts or range of information that are important for you to know. Others have been made deliberately difficult, turning on very specific details, in order to draw you back to the book. You can use the section as a simple review test to check your knowledge, but you will get more out of it by using it as a more active study guide. Pay as much attention to the answers that you don't select as the ones that you do, plan on going back to the book to find the answers, and don't stop yourself from re-reading other things that draw your attention while you're there.

   4. *Guide to Documents:* Each chapter contains questions related to the documents used in *The Western Experience*. In general, the first question is a multiple choice question focusing on your comprehension of the main point of the document. The second is then an "essay" style question calling for broader interpretive thought and showing how the document might be used to increase historical understanding and gain insights into historical questions.

5. *Significant Individuals:* Here, the principal historical figures mentioned in the text are listed, along with some brief biographical information. This is intended to be used in two ways: first, as an exercise; and second, as a reference. The section is structured as two columns, with the names in a numbered list on the left, and the descriptions in a lettered list on the right. Note that the names are NOT next to the correct description. The first thing you need to do is the exercise of matching the name to the correct description. You can do this while you are reading or afterwards, and either by drawing a line from the name to the description or by writing the description's letter next to the name. Once all the names and descriptions have been matched, you can use the list as a reference when you study.

6. *Chronological Diagram:* This diagram is intended to be used as a reference. Note what different sorts of events are related chronologically. It is often useful to compare the chronological chart in one chapter with those in the preceding and succeeding chapters. On an even broader scale, this is done in the chronological diagrams contained in each section summary.

7. *Identification:* Some of the most important developments and events in the chapter are listed here. It is set up exactly like the Significant Individuals section, and you can use it in the same ways.

8. *Map Exercises:* In most chapters maps are provided with exercises that relate to some of the main concerns of the chapter. Standing alone and without directly using the text, some of these exercises are difficult. But by utilizing the maps already present in the text and in some cases specific sections of the text referred to in the exercise, they become easier. The purposes here are to help you get used to using maps, to emphasize the importance of geographic considerations in history, and to encourage you to picture developments described in the text in concrete, geographic terms.

9. *Problems for Analysis:* These are designed to cover each of the main sections of the chapter. They require a combination of specific information and analysis. Working on these problems should give you a much stronger grasp of the materials and issues dealt with in each section of the chapter. In addition, you might use some of these problems to prepare for class discussions. They might help you formulate questions to ask in class or present a point of view that you find particularly interesting or irritating.

10. *Speculations:* These constitute unusual, interesting questions. They may require you to put yourself back into history, compare the past with the present, or speculate on various historical alternatives. They might be used as a first step toward identifying a paper topic or developing a classroom debate. From aspects of broader speculations, more specific historical problems could be identified, put into perspective, and dealt with.

11. *Transitions:* These relate the previous chapter, the present chapter, and the following chapter. One of the main purposes here is to help you avoid losing the continuity of history; each chapter in the text is integrally connected to what came before and what follows. Another purpose is to emphasize briefly the main arguments presented in the chapter; focusing on specific events can sometimes lead one to overlook the broader conclusions that are being drawn.

11. *Answers:* The answers to all multiple choice questions are given at the end of each chapter. You can use these answers in three ways. (1) If you want, you can simply come to this section, mark the answers near the questions, and use the exercises as a reference. (2) You can answer the questions from memory to test yourself, and then come here to see how well you did. Study the sections were you get question wrong particularly carefully. (3) You can avoid this section as much as possible by referring back to the book to check your answers or help find the answers you know you don't know. Only check here to make sure you have come up with the right answer on your own. This is probably the most effective way to use the multiple choice questions and matching exercises as an aid to your studies.

In addition to the chapters, there are three section summaries. These correspond to periods into which historians commonly divide Western history and to sections of the book often covered in an exam or a paper. Each contains Chronological Diagrams, Map Exercises, and Box Charts for you to fill in. Tabulating material from your reading notes on these charts (which you will need to reproduce in larger format in your notebook or on separate sheets of paper) will help you place individuals and events in a broader thematic and chronological framework and distinguish important facts from less important ones. Note that the charts are structured according to the categories discussed above in order to give you a standard frame of reference into which to fit the history of Western Civilization. The authors discuss these categories in the introduction to the textbook, and have organized the index to make it relatively easy to access material on each topic. The charts should be particularly useful when you are reviewing for an exam.

Dennis Sherman
Edward Bever

CHAPTER HIGHLIGHTS

1. Humans became food producers rather than food gatherers some 12,000 years ago with the development of agriculture, the essential step in the creation of complex civilizations.

2. As cities were established in the river valleys of Mesopotamia, the early Sumerian and Babylonian civilizations emerged.

3. Egyptians developed a prosperous, long-lasting, religious society along the Nile between about 3000 and 300 B.C.

4. After 1650 the Hittites established a powerful state in the Near East, but between 1250 and 1100, invaders utilizing iron weapons ended the Hittite domination and brought the Bronze Age to an end.

5. In Palestine, the Phoenicians created a sophisticated urban civilization, while the Israelites developed a short-lived kingdom but an enduring religious and cultural tradition.

6. The Assyrians—followed by the Chaldeans, the Medes, and the Persians—established powerful unifying empires in the Near East.

CHAPTER OUTLINE

I. The Earliest Humans

1. Human Beings as Food Gatherers

2. Human Beings as Food Producers

3. Early Near Eastern Villages

II. The First Civilizations in Mesopotamia

1. The Emergence of Civilization

2. Sumer

3. The Babylonian Kingdom

4. Mesopotamian Culture

III. Egypt

1. The Old and Middle Kingdoms

2. The New Kingdom

3. A View of Egyptian Society

IV. The Early Indo-Europeans

1. The Hittite Kingdom

2. The Close of the Bronze Age

V. Palestine

1. Canaanites and Phoenicians

2. Hebrew Society and the Bible

3. The Jewish Legacy

VI. The Near Eastern Empires

1. The Assyrian State

2. The Chaldeans and the Medes

3. The Persian Empire

SELF TEST

1. The earliest ancestors of humans probably appeared in Africa around

   a.. 2,000,000 years ago.

   b. 1,250,000 years ago.

   c. 350,000 years ago.

   d. 40,000 years ago.

2. Early (Old Stone Age) humans did all of the following EXCEPT

   a. get their food by hunting and gathering.

   b. divide some types of work between women and men.

   c. develop pottery and weaving.

   d. make paintings of wild animals.

3. The agricultural revolution, planting crops and herding animals, had all of the following effects EXCEPT

   a. supporting a larger population.

   b. encouraging new skills and specialties.

   c. necessitating long term planning.

   d. promoting the concept of male "father" deities.

4. The first agricultural villages appeared in the hills of the Near East because

   a. the humans with sufficiently advanced brains were only found here.

   b. the region offered the necessary combination of animals for domestication and vegetables and cereals.

   c. the area's dry climate necessitated large-scale irrigation projects.

   d. the hills provided protection from less developed hunting and gathering peoples.

5. The appearance of civilization around 3000 B.C. brought all of the following EXCEPT

   a. the end to the period of extensive reliance on slavery.

   b. the creations of laws and legal codes.

   c. complex social organization based on occupational specialization.

   d. establishment of priesthoods.

6. The geography of Mesopotamia influenced Sumerian civilization in all the following ways EXCEPT

   a. the rich alluvial plain supported an abundant agriculture.

   b. the lack of timber and stone forced it to develop trading to obtain these necessary materials.

   c. the region's isolation led Sumerians to see themselves as unique.

   d. vulnerability to floods and invasions created a strain of pessimism in Sumerian thought.

7. After around 2000 B.C., the Babylonian Kingdom established its control over lower Mesopotamia, subduing or destroying the Sumerian city states. The greatest of the Babylonian kings was:

   a. Sargon the Great.

   b. Hammurabi.

   c. Ur-Nammu.

   d. Amorites.

8. The early Mesopotamians developed all of the following EXCEPT:

   a. writing.

   b. mathematics.

   c. astronomy.

   d. monotheism.

9. The geography of Egypt influenced Egyptian civilization in all the following ways EXCEPT

   a. the dependability of the Nile's annual floods and the equability of the climate contributed to Egyptians' optimistic attitudes toward life and death.

   b. the looming presence of mountains inspired the Egyptians to build great pyramids.

   c. the narrowness of the Nile valley and the presence of the river running through it contributed to early and strong political centralization.

   d. Egypt's isolation from other peoples allowed a long, generally unbroken development.

10. All of the following characterized Egypt during the Old Kingdom EXCEPT

    a. domination of both the government and the economy by a god-king.

    b. notable political and social stability.

    c. concept of "right order" reflecting the will of Aton, the supreme sun god.

    d. a rich literature including religious myths, instructions on how to get ahead, fables, and love poems.

11. The Egyptian New Kingdom, or Empire, strengthened its control over the nobles in order to create a powerful military state that extended its power beyond the Nile Valley into Palestine and Syria. The New Kingdom arose in response to the rule of which people:

    a. the Hyksos.

    b. the Hittites.

    c. the Hebrews.

    d. the Hellenes.

3

12. All of the following characterized Egyptian society EXCEPT:

    a. education offered the chance to rise through service in the government hierarchy.

    b. women had the right to own property, initiate legal action, and enter the priesthood.

    c. children were valued as security for the future.

    d. the economic difference between free citizens and slaves was vast.

13. The Indo-European peoples were related by

    a. a common origin in the Indian sub-continent.

    b. a common ancestral language.

    c. similar techniques of cultivation, government, and warfare.

    d. common features including stature, skin color, and brain size.

14. The Hittite kingdom concluded the first known non-aggression pact with

    a. Egypt.

    b. Babylonia.

    c. Assyria.

    d. Mitanni.

15. Iron has been called the "democratic metal" because

    a. iron miners were the first workers vital enough to be able to secure a voice in government.

    b. iron tools increased agricultural efficiency so much that differences in wealth decreased.

    c. cheap iron weapons enabled more men to become warriors, able to demand a voice in government.

    d. iron machinery was cheaper than slave labor, resulting in the gradual disappearance of slavery.

16. The Phoenicians accomplished all of the following EXCEPT

    a. establishing a centralized, sea-based colonial empire.

    b. reportedly sailing around Africa for the first time.

    c. creating the first phonetic alphabet.

    d. creating a sophisticate urban civilization.

17. One way that the Hebrew religion was innovative was that it emphasized

    a. ethical conduct.

    b. the equality of all people.

    c. the need for a strong king.

    d. rituals to control nature.

18. The chief legacies of the Hebrews to Western Civilization were

    a. traditions of strong tribal monarchy and national unity.

    b. belief in a single God and ethical laws.

    c. prophetic traditions of social criticism and moral reform.

    d. the ideas of women's equality and the rights of children.

19. The Assyrians accomplished all of the following EXCEPT

    a.   unifying the Near East and Egypt for the first time.

    b.   introducing Aramaic as a common language throughout their empire.

    c.   creating magnificent works of art.

    d.   suppressing rebelliousness among subject peoples.

20. The Chaldeans and the Medes

    a.   shared the glory in conquering the Assyrians.

    b.   left voluminous records of their daily life.

    c.   divided the Mesopotamian territories of the Assyrians.

    d.   cooperated in mammoth astronomical projects.

21. The primary accomplishment of the Persian Empire was to

    a.   promote an expansion of trade amounting to a "commercial revolution."

    b.   unify the Nile, Mesopotamian, and Indus valleys into a single state.

    c.   create the most highly centralized state since the Old Kingdom of Egypt.

    d.   subdue the Greek city-states around the Aegean Sea.

GUIDE TO DOCUMENTS

I. Hammurabi's Law Code

1. What is the primary principle of justice reflected in these laws?

    a.   Compassion.

    b.   Retribution.

    c.   Compensation.

    d.   Reconciliation.

2. What do these laws reveal about the rights of women in Babylonia?

II. The Salvation of Israel

1. What does this document reveal about the Israelite perception of God?

    a.   God is merciful.

    b.   God is mighty.

    c.   God is cruel.

    d.   God is unknowable.

2. What does the passage reveal about God's relationship to the Israelites?

    a.   He favors them.

    b.   He is angered by them.

    c.   He is proud of them.

    d.   He relies on them.

3. How does this document explain the escape of the Israelites from Egypt? How might this explanation be evaluated?

III. Jeremiah Reproaches Israel

1. Compare this document with the previous document on the salvation of Israel. How does this document add to our understanding of the Israelite perception of God?

   a. God is just.

   b. God is stern.

   c. God is all-powerful.

   d. God is unfathomable.

2. What does this reveal about the sorts of problems experienced by the people of Israel?

SIGNIFICANT INDIVIDUALS

Match the name with the description

1. Gilgamesh   a. Lawgiving Hebrew prophet (ca. 1270)

2. Sargon   b. Founder of Persian empire (559–530)

3. Hammurabi (HAM-uh-rah-bē)   c. First great warlord in Western history, ruler of Akkad (2371–2316)

4. Menes (or Narmer)   d. King of Egypt who promoted worship of the sun god (1369?–1353?)

5. Hatshepsut (hat-SHEP-soot)   e. Opulent King of Chaldea, (604–562)

6. Amenhotep IV (ah-muhn-HŎ-tep) (or Akhnaton)   f. Lawgiving King of Babylonia, (1792–1750)

7. Ramses II   g. King of Persia and it's greatest administrator (521–486)

8. Saul   h. King who unified Upper and Lower Egypt (ca. 3000)

9. Moses   i. Greatest King of Israel (1010?–960?)

10. David   j. Last powerful Assyrian King (668–627?)

11. Ashurbanipal (ah-shoor-BAH-nuh-pahl)   k. Legendary King of Sumer (ca. 2700)

12. Nebuchadnezzar (NAB-oo-kuhd-nez-uhr)   l. Female king of Egypt (1512-1482)

13. Cyrus (SĪ-rus)   m. Persian priest and reformer (ca. 600),

14. Darius   n. Egyptian king who fought the Hittites and built the temple at Karnak (1292–1225)

15. Zoroaster (or Zarathustra)   o. First King of Israel (ca. 1020)

IDENTIFICATION

Match the name with the description

1. Homo Sapiens
   (HŌ-mō SĀ-pē-enz)

2. Neolithic Age (NĚ-e-LITH-ik)

3. Bronze Age

4. Mesopotamia
   (MES-e-pe-TĀ-me-e)

5. ziggurat (ZIG-uh-rat)

6. cuneiform (kyoo-NĚ-uh-form)

7. Code of Hammurabi

8. Nile

9. *maat* (muh-AHT)

10. hieroglyphics (hī-ruh-GLIF-iks)

11. Indo-European

12. Yahweh (YAH-wā)

13. Ten Commandments

14. Zoroastrianism
    (zor-ō-AS-trē-uh-niz-uhm)

15. Ahura Mazda
    (ah-HOOR-uh MAZ-duh)

a. Language group from which most modern European languages descend.

b. Egyptian system of writing combining pictographs and phonetic signs

c. Persian supreme god of good

d. River flowing through Egypt

e. Sumerian temple

f. The "New Stone Age" of the agricultural revolution

g. Persian religion based on struggle between good and evil

h. "Thinking human beings"

i. Ethical code of conduct of Hebrew religion

j. Hebrew god

k. Period when the best tools were made from a combination of copper and other metals

l. Egyptian concept of "right order"

m. River valley where civilization first appeared

n. Mesopotamian writing with wedge shaped marks in clay

o. Compilation of Babylonian laws

CHRONOLOGICAL DIAGRAM

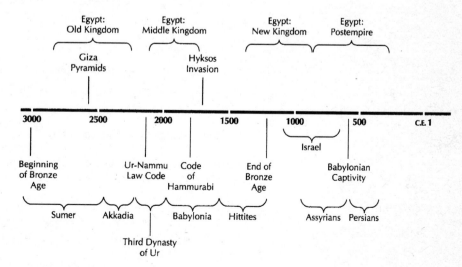

7

MAP EXERCISES

1. Locate areas where early civilizations arose.

2. Show the direction where major invaders came from.

3. Show areas of likely interaction between civilizations.

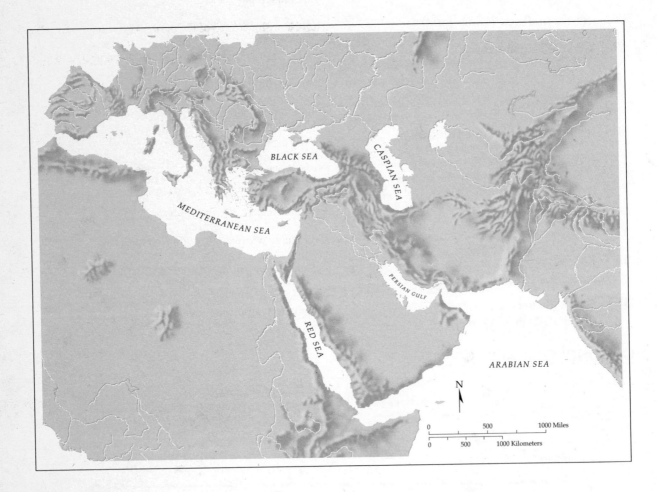

1. Indicate the approximate boundaries of Egypt, the Assyrian Empire, the Hittite kingdom, the Hebrew kingdom, and the Persian Empire at their heights.

2. Indicate the main river valleys in the area

3. Indicate the location of some early agricultural sites.

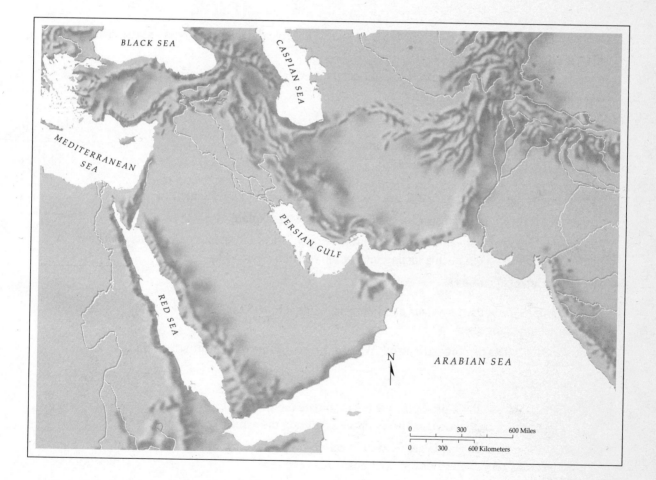

PROBLEMS FOR ANALYSIS

I. The Earliest Humans

1. Why was the development of agriculture so crucial for the establishment of civilization? What advantages do food producers have over food gatherers?
2. What is known about gender roles during the Paleolithic and Neolithic Ages, and what is speculation?

II. The First Civilizations in Mesopotamia

1. In what ways was the rise of Sumerian cities a significant development in Western history? Describe the characteristics of Sumerian civilization.
2. How has analysis of cuneiform inscriptions and codes revealed much about Babylonian politics, society, and culture?

III. Egypt

1. Compare Egyptian civilization with Mesopotamia. What role did geography play in the different development of the two civilizations?
2. What do Egyptian attitudes toward life after death reveal about the Egyptian religion and attitudes toward life in general?

IV. The Early Indo-Europeans

1. Why was the introduction of iron so important?

V. Palestine

1. What explains the extraordinary influence of the Canaanites and Phoenicians?
2. How useful is the Old Testament as a historical document? Explain.
3. What were the major innovations of the Hebrew religion? How did older civilizations contribute to them? Why did they exert such a lasting impact on Western Civilization?

VI. The Near Eastern Empires

1. Using examples from the Assyrians and Persians, explain how Near Eastern kings were able to hold their vast empires together.
2. What were the tenets of Zoroastrianism? What did it contribute to the Christian religion?

SPECULATIONS

1. Explain what you think prompted people to initiate the first civilizations. How do you explain the development of civilizations in different places during the same period of time?
2. What advantages do people get from civilization? What do they lose? Use examples from Egyptian and Near Eastern civilizations in your answer.
3. Given the historical conditions of the time, if you were a Persian king in the year 550, how would you organize your empire? Why?

TRANSITIONS

In "The First Civilizations," the nature and beginnings of Western civilization in the Near East and Egypt are examined. The development of agriculture in these river valleys was the crucial step allowing greater numbers of people to support themselves, enabling the production of surplus food, facilitating specialization, and stimulating the growth of more complex societies. These changes were furthered through the growth of cities and imperial expansion, consolidating the transition to civilized conditions. Early civilizations discovered different ways to deal with the problems of how people relate to each other and to divine forces. Some of the peoples in this area—such as the Egyptians, Assyrians, and Persians—developed large and long-lasting societies; while others, such as the Israelites, left a more influential religious and ethical heritage.

In "The Forming of Greek Civilization," the focus will shift north to Greece, where a highly urbanized and extraordinarily sophisticated civilization developed.

ANSWERS

Self Test

1a; 2c; 3d; 4b; 5a; 6c; 7b; 8d; 9b; 10c; 11a; 12d; 13b; 14a; 15c; 16a; 17a; 18b; 19d; 20a; 21b

Guide to Documents

I-1b; II-1b; II-2a; III-1b

Significant Individuals

1k; 2c; 3f; 4h; 5l; 6d; 7n; 8o; 9a; 10i; 11j; 12e; 13b; 14g; 15m

Identification

1h; 2f; 3k; 4m; 5e; 6n; 7o; 8d; 9l; 10b; 11a; 12j; 13i; 14g; 15c

TWO

THE FORMING OF GREEK CIVILIZATION

CHAPTER HIGHLIGHTS

1.   Early Greek civilization was dominated by Crete (the Minoan civilization) and independent city-states (most prominently, Mycenae). This age was brought to a close by the Dorian invasions around 1100, which ushered in a Dark Age of some 300 years.

2.   Greek civilization revived after 800, as indicated by the flowering of Homeric epic poetry, the establishment of numerous Greek colonies, the development of an unusual religion, and the creation of uniquely Hellenic literature and art.

3.   Greek political, social, and economic life was centered around the *polis,* whose organization and government evolved into different forms over time. The two most prominent city-states were Sparta and Athens.

4.   The Greeks unified themselves and gained stunning victories over the invading Persians, thereby preserving their independence.

5.   After the Persian Wars, Athens rose to dominance in the Greek world, attaining its height during the Age of Pericles.

6.   The Peloponnesian War proved disastrous for Athens and many other Greek city-states.

CHAPTER OUTLINE

I. Crete and Early Greece (Ca. 3000–1100 B.C.)

1. Cretan Civilization

2. Crete and the Greeks

3. Mycenaean Civilization (Ca. 1600–1100 B.C.)

II. The Greek Renaissance (Ca. 800–600 B.C.)

1. Greek Religion

2. Public Games

3. Colonization (Ca. 750–550 B.C.)

4. The Alphabet

5. Archaic Literature

III. The Polis

1. Organization and Government

2. The Economy of the Poleis (Ca. 700–400 B.C.)

3. Sparta and Athens (Ca. 700–500 B.C.)

IV. The Challenge of Persia

1. The Invasion under Darius and Marathon (490 B.C.)

2. The Second Persian War (480–479 B.C.)

V. The Wars of the Fifth Century (479–404 B.C.)

1. The Athenian Empire

2. The Age of Pericles

3. The Peloponnesian War (431–404 B.C.)

SELF TEST

1. All of the following characterized Cretan civilization EXCEPT

    a. it was peaceful.

    b. its wealth came from trade.

    c. women enjoyed relatively high status.

    d. it ruled a wide empire.

2. Cretan civilization influenced all of the following aspects of Greek civilization EXCEPT

    a. art.

    b. government.

    c. religion.

    d. writing.

3. Geography influenced Mycenaean Civilization because

    a. mountains divide Greece into many small valleys that led the Greeks to develop independent states.

    b. the country's climate led the Greeks to live close together in a few large settlements.

    c. living in the mountains made the Greeks particularly independent, and thus unwilling to live under kings.

    d. the unstable geology of the region made the Mycenaeans particularly vulnerable to natural disasters.

4. The Greek Renaissance from 800 to 600 was characterized by all of the following EXCEPT

    a. poetry and art broke new frontiers.

    b. the economy expanded.

    c. Mycenaean Civilization was restored.

    d. the *polis*, or independent city-state, emerged

5. Greek religion was characterized by all of the following EXCEPT

    a. the anthropomorphic gods intervened frequently in human affairs.

    b. the religion prescribed rigid standards of moral conduct.

    c. priests and priestesses exercised little political power.

    d. each city had as its patron one god from the pantheon common to all Greeks.

6. The Olympic games in ancient Greece were

    a. contests among amateur athletes for honor.

    b. a source of fame and riches for the winners.

    c. held in honor of the goddess Athena.

    d. held once every four years on Mt. Olympus.

7. The Greeks coped with population pressures after 750 B.C. by

    a. selling poor farmers into slavery.

    b. exporting population to independent colonies overseas.

    c. establishing colonial empires.

    d. conquering neighboring peoples and driving them from their land.

8. Adoption of an alphabet was important for the ancient Greeks because

    a. it became the basis for later alphabets in both Western and Eastern Europe.

    b. it gave them a decisive advantage in trade over the Phoenicians.

    c. laws could be made readily available, facilitating public involvement in government.

    d. it was used in making monuments to their victories, enhancing the citizens' pride in their cities.

9. Archaic Greek literature was particularly innovative because

    a. Greek authors began to use literature as a form of frank self-expression.

    b. it exalted a benevolent God whose primary concern was ethical conduct among humans.

    c. it was the first literature to use rhymed verse.

    d. it was used to narrate the stories of the gods in their endless struggles against one another.

10. All of the following are true about the Greek *poleis* EXCEPT

    a. they were city-states consisting of an urban center and the surrounding farm country.

    b. originally ruled by kings, by 700 they were dominated by landowning aristocrats.

    c. in the seventh and sixth centuries, ordinary people gained a greater role in government.

    d. at the end of the sixth century tyrants emerged as champions of the traditional aristocracy.

11. All of the following were true about the economy of the *poleis* EXCEPT

    a. the primary activity was agriculture.

    b. because of the poor soil, Greeks also engaged in fishing and trade.

    c. slaves played a vital role in the economy.

    d. industry was well advanced, with shops employing 300 or more workers.

12. Sparta and Athens differed in all of the following ways EXCEPT

    a. Sparta was a closed, militaristic society, while Athens was a cosmopolitan, commercial center.

    b. Sparta's army made it the dominant land power, while Athens' fleet made it the leading sea power.

    c. Sparta pursued an aggressively expansionist policy, while Athens protected other cities' independence.

    d. Sparta was a monarchy, while Athens was a democracy.

13. The Persian King Darius attacked Athens because

    a.   it had helped Greek cities in Ionia revolt against his rule.

    b.   he coveted the city's trading wealth.

    c.   the independent Greek cities posed a critical threat to the survival of his empire.

    d.   Athens had seized the city of Marathon from him.

14. The Greeks won the critical battle of Salamis because

    a.   they had raised a bigger army than Persia.

    b.   a handful of Spartan soldiers were able to defeat the main Persian force.

    c.   Athens had created a powerful fleet.

    d.   they captured the Persian king Xerxes through a clever ruse.

15. After successfully leading the Greek resistance to Persia, Athens

    a.   concentrated on developing peaceful trade relations around the Aegean Sea.

    b.   returned to its perennial isolation.

    c.   gradually transformed the Delian League into an empire.

    d.   turned on Sparta to secure its primacy in the Greek world..

16. All of the following are true of the Athenian statesman Pericles EXCEPT

    a.   he secured Athens' dominance of the Greek world.

    b.   he sponsored construction of the greatest Greek temple, the Parthenon.

    c.   he dominated Athens through its democratic institutions.

    d.   he never held high civil office.

17. Athenian policy during the Peloponnesian War was characterized by

    a.   careful planning and meticulous execution by cautious professionals.

    b.   rash actions advocated by demagogues supported by popular enthusiasm.

    c.   scrupulous regard for the rights of neutral powers.

    d.   a steadfast refusal to make even temporary truces with the enemy.

18. The most important consequence of the Peloponnesian War was that

    a.   Athens emerged as the undisputed leader of Greece.

    b.   Sparta's victory propelled it to lasting domination of Greece.

    c.   the war left Greece exhausted and demoralized.

    d.   Persia was able to take advantage of Greek divisions to complete its conquest.

GUIDE TO DOCUMENTS

I. The Debate over Black Athena

1. Bernal makes all of the following points EXCEPT

    a. the Greek language was formed at a time when Egyptian influence was at its height.

    b. Greek is an Indo-European language, but it contains a strong admixture of non-Indo-European words.

    c. many Greek religious beliefs are similar to older Egyptian beliefs.

    d. archaeological evidence proves that Egypto-Semitic conquerors long dominated Crete.

2. Lefkowitz's primary criticism of Bernal is that

    a. he has not offered conclusive proofs of his argument.

    b. his argument is based on Herodotus, whose information is known to be inaccurate.

    c. his theory would require a dramatic change in our understanding of the origins of Greek culture.

    d. he has not sharpened the quality of the debate about the origins of Greek culture.

3. Many people consider this scholarly debate extraordinarily important. Why do you think this is so?

II. Sappho's Love Poetry

1. What does this reveal about romantic love in Greek civilization?

    a. That the strongest love existed between women and women.

    b. That true love could only exist between men and women.

    c. That for Greeks the bodily seat of love was in the heart.

    d. That the Greeks experienced love only as a sexual sensation.

2. Does this provide good evidence for the position of women in Greek civilization?

III. "They Have a Master Called Law"

1. What, according to this work by Herodotus, was the Greek view of the difference between rule by a man and rule by law?

    a. Rule by man is based on fear, while rule by law is based on loyalty.

    b. Free men fear the law more than subjects fear their master.

    c. Men who follow the law cannot be beaten by men who follow a man.

    d. Rule by law is unique to the Greeks.

2. What seems to be the message of the Spartan Demaratus? Should what he says about the Spartans be considered valid for all Greeks?

SIGNIFICANT INDIVIDUALS

Match the name with the description

1. Homer

2. Hesiod (HĒ-si-od)

3. Archilochus of Paros (ahr-KIL-uh-kuhs)

4. Lycurgus (lī-KUR-gus)

5. Draco

6. Sappho of Lesbos

7. Solon

8. Pisistratus (pī-SIS-truh-tuhs)

9. Cleisthenes (KLĬS-the-nēz)

10. Darius

11. Xerxes (ZURK-sēz)

12. Pericles

13. Alcibiades (al-si-BĬ-a-dez)

a. Persian king who led first invasion of Greece (521–486)

b. Earliest Athenian lawgiver (ca. 621)

c. Athenian statesman who led the disastrous attack on Syracuse (450?–404)

d. Athenian tyrant who championed the poor (590?–527)

e. Author of the *Illiad* and the *Odyssey* (8th century?)

f. Founder of Athenian democracy (ca. 508)

g. Female lyric poet (ca. 600)

h. Leader of Athens during its Golden Age (490?-429)

i. Legendary Spartan lawgiver

j. Persian king defeated in Second Persian War (486-465)

k. Lyric poet who specialized in self-revelation (ca. 650)

l. Social critic and genealogist of the gods (ca. 700)

m. Reformer of Athens' economy (ca. 630-ca. 559)

CHRONOLOGICAL DIAGRAMS

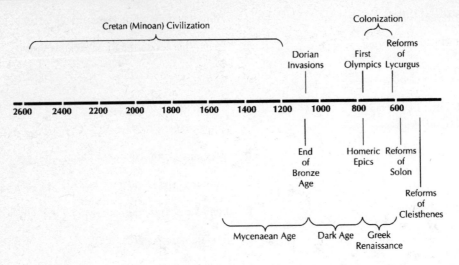

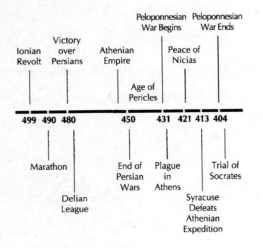

IDENTIFICATION

1. Knossos (NOS-us)
2. Linear B
3. Trojan War
4. Dorian invasion
5. the *Illiad*
6. Panhellenic games
7. Polis (PŌ-lis)
8. "Tyrants"
9. Helots (HĒL-uhtz)
10. Phalanx (Fā-langks))
11. *Demokratia* (dem-o-KRA-tē-uh)
12. Council of 500
13. Ionian revolt
14. Salamis
15. Delian League (DĒ-li-an)
16. Trireme (TRĪ-rēm)

a. Athletic competitions open to all Greeks
b. Event that led to the First Persian War
c. Popular leaders who overturned rule of the old aristocracy
d. Rowed warships used to smash and sink enemy vessels
e. Naval battle won by the Greeks against the Persians
f. Close-packed formation of soldiers
g. Mycenaean Age war immortalized by Homer
h. Site of most majestic Cretan palace
i. Athenian body that prepared business for the assembly
j. Enslaved Messenians who worked for the Spartans
k. The Dark Age movement of peoples into Greece
l. Rule by the mass of citizens
m. Epic poem that explored aristocratic military values
n. Military alliance dominated by Athens
o. A self-governing city-state
p. System of writing used to record an early form of Greek

MAP EXERCISES

1.   Indicate the approximate location of Mycenae, Crete, Troy, Sparta, Athens, Ionia, Miletus, Peloponnese, Attica, and the Aegean Sea.

2.   Compare this map with those in Chapter 1. Describe the geographic differences, and indicate how these might relate to differences between the societies of the Near East and those of Greece.

1. Indicate (by shading) the principal Athenian and Spartan allies during the Peloponnesian War.

PROBLEMS FOR ANALYSIS

I. Crete and Early Greece

1. Compare the Cretan and Mycenaean civilizations. What evidence is there for contact between these two civilizations?

2. In what ways did Greece enter a Dark Age between 1100 and 800? Was this an unmitigated disaster? Why?

II. The Greek Renaissance

1. Analyze the religious and cultural importance of the Homeric epics.

2. In what ways did colonization lead to significant changes in Greek economic, social, and political life?

3. How do the main themes of Archaic literature relate to the concerns of modern life?

III. The Polis

1. How was the polis organized?

2. Compare Sparta and Athens. What were the advantages and disadvantages of the various political and social choices these two city-states made?

3. Trace the development of more democratic institutions in Athens. What were the main problems in shaping this development?

IV. The Challenge of Persia

1. How do you explain the Greek victory over the Persians, despite the overwhelming odds?

V. The Wars of the Fifth Century

1. How was Athens able to rise to such a position of leadership in the Greek world? How did its role in the Persian War contribute to this? How important was Pericles?

2. Considering that Athens survived and remained independent, what was so particularly disastrous about the Peloponnesian War?

3. What does Athens' conduct before and during the Peloponnesian war suggest about the nature of democracy?

SPECULATIONS

1. How do you explain the development of such an extraordinary civilization by the Greeks? Do you think much of the credit belongs to some sort of Greek "spirit," or were geographic factors more important?

2. Should Greek civilization be considered superior to Near Eastern civilizations, or simply different? How do you evaluate this?

TRANSITIONS

In "The First Civilizations," the origins of Western civilizations in the Near East and Egypt were examined.

In "The Forming of Greek Civilization," focus is shifted to the Aegean area. The Greeks viewed the world and human affairs in extraordinarily natural, rational, and secular terms. Greek philosophy helped create a common cultural tradition for the Western experience. Living in independent city-states, Greeks experienced changing political forms, democracy eventually spreading to an unprecedented degree. The evolution of Greek civilization, from the Minoans and Mycenaeans to the Spartans and Athenians, is traced, with emphasis on the later political developments in Athens and cultural accomplishments.

In "Classical and Hellenistic Greece," developments in Greece and the Near East during the fifth, fourth, and third centuries will be examined.

ANSWERS

Self Test

1d; 2b; 3a; 4c; 5b; 6b; 7b; 8c; 9a; 10d; 11d; 12c; 13a; 14c; 15c; 16a; 17b; 18c

Guide to Documents

I-1d; I-2a; II-1c; III-1b

Significant Individuals

1e; 2l; 3k; 4i; 5b; 6g; 7m; 8d; 9f; 10a; 11j; 12h; 13c

Identification

1h; 2p; 3g; 4k; 5m; 6a; 7o; 8c; 9j; 10f; 11l; 12i; 13b; 14e; 15n; 16d

THREE
CLASSICAL AND HELLENISTIC GREECE

CHAPTER HIGHLIGHTS

1. Athens produced extraordinarily creative dramatists, historians, architects, sculptors, and philosophers during the Classical Age (500–323).

2. Philip II and Alexander took advantage of the disunity among the Greek city-states and brought Macedonia to dominance in Greece. Alexander led a force that conquered the Persian Empire.

3. The period between the death of Alexander and that of Cleopatra is called the Hellenistic Age, a period of large warring kingdoms, great cities, relative prosperity, and important cultural accomplishments.

CHAPTER OUTLINE

I. Classical Greek Culture (Ca. 500–323 B.C.)

1. Greek Tragedy

2. Comedy

3. Historical Writing

4. Philosophy

5. The Roles of Women

II. The Rise of Macedonia

1. The Weaknesses of the Poleis

2. Philip II of Macedonia

3. Alexander the Great

III. The Hellenistic Age (323–130 B.C.)

1. The Dissolution of Alexander's Empire

2. Economic Life

3. Literature, Art, and Science

4. Philosophy and Religion

SELF TEST

1. Drawing of the familiar tales and characters of mythology, Greek dramatists dealt with all of the following themes EXCEPT

    a. the nature of justice.

    b. the frustration of love by social prejudice.

    c. the tragedy of a strong person caught in the grip of fate

    d. how the workings of the mind and emotions shape individual destiny.

2. Aristophanes' comedies were

   a. pure entertainments.

   b. social and political satires.

   c. warm explorations of love and sexuality.

   d. covert defenses of the status quo in Greek society.

3. Greek historians were distinguished by their

   a. objective investigation into the causes of events.

   b. reliance on older sources from the Near East.

   c. partisan point of view.

   d. focus on the economic structures underlying political events.

4. Greek philosophy began from the assumption that

   a. the gods' behavior is rational and can therefore be understood through reason.

   b. the universe and humans' place within it can only be understood through revelation.

   c. numbers are the key to understanding of the structure of the universe.

   d. there is an order in the universe that humans can discover through reason.

5. The earliest Greek philosophers in Miletus focused on determining

   a. the proper relationship between humans and the gods.

   b. how a person should conduct him or herself in the world.

   c. the ideal constitution for a state.

   d. the fundamental composition of the universe.

6. Pythagoras' assertion that mathematical relationships are the key to understanding the universe

   a. led to his trial and death sentence in Athens.

   b. presaged the use of mathematical models in modern science.

   c. enabled him to create some of the most beautiful harmonies in musical history.

   d. were based on experiments by contemporary Greek physicists.

7. The Sophists taught their students

   a. how to achieve success in life.

   b. how to discover moral absolutes.

   c. to support revealed truths through reason.

   d. how to achieve happiness by renouncing the world..

8. Socrates' primary legacy was

   a. proving that knowledge inevitably leads to morally right choices.

   b. educating elitists who betrayed Athens during its struggle against Sparta.

   c. pursuing moral truths through a process of questioning and logical analysis.

   d. showing that the truly virtuous person need not fear death.

9. Socrates' pupil Plato regarded the material world as

   a. a reflection of the eternal forms that constitute true reality.

   b. the only aspect of reality that is truly knowable.

   c. composed of water, echoing Babylonian myths of a primeval flood.

   d. an illusion caused by the play of shadows on the wall of a cave.

10. Plato's pupil Aristotle differed from his teacher in that he

   a. taught students about his philosophy.

   b. developed an explicit philosophy of government.

   c. focused on understanding the material world.

   d. regarded reason as the ultimate means of gaining knowledge.

11. All of the following were true about respectable women in Greece EXCEPT

   a. they were always under the control of a male.

   b. they were either confined to the house or chaperoned.

   c. they normally married as teenagers to much older men.

   d. they were regarded as more self-controlled than men.

12. After the Pelopennesian War, the Greek city-states were weakened by

   a. natural disasters.

   b. economic depression.

   c. chronic warfare.

   d. Persian subversion.

13. Phillip II of Macedonia used all of the following to establish control over Greece EXCEPT

   a. careful diplomacy.

   b. a powerful army.

   c. well-timed leniency.

   d. economic pressure.

14. What made Alexander the Great great was that he

   a. extended Greek rule over the entire civilized world between Greece and India.

   b. created a lasting, unified empire fusing Greek, Persian, and Indian influences.

   c. founded the city of Alexandria as a link between Egypt and Greece.

   d. liberated the peoples of the Persian empire and returned them to self-government.

15. The successor states after Alexander's empire broke up were characterized by all of the following EXCEPT

   a. Greek rulers.

   b. strong armies.

   c. large bureaucracies.

   d. democratic governments.

16. The Hellenistic economy was characterized by all of the following EXCEPT

    a.   the scale of economic activity was far greater than heretofore.

    b.   agriculture ceased to be the dominant activity.

    c.   long-distance trade grew enormously.

    d.   economic development supported the growth of magnificent cities.

17. All of the following characterized Hellenistic culture EXCEPT

    a.   the most significant literary achievements were in scholarship.

    b.   music developed an austere simplicity that distinguished it from earlier forms.

    c.   architecture and sculpture became grandiose, emotional, and realistic.

    d.   advances were made in mathematics and science that would not be surpassed for centuries.

18. Epicurianism taught that

    a.   we should act in accordance with nature and reason in order to lead a virtuous life.

    b.   we should concern ourselves with leading pleasurable lives, avoiding physical and mental pain..

    c.   because life is transitory, we should seek the maximum possible stimulation in the time we have.

    d.   because life is transitory, we should make what contribution we can while we have the time.

19. The Stoics taught all of the following EXCEPT

    a.   we should act in accordance with nature and reason in order to lead a virtuous life.

    b.   we should be compassionate and tolerant, for all humanity is part of a universal family.

    c.   we should never give in to adversity, but instead constantly struggle to overcome it.

    d.   we should balance participation in public life with satisfaction of our private needs.

20. The mystery religions of the Hellenistic world involved all of the following EXCEPT

    a.   worship of a savior whose death and resurrection would redeem the sins of humanity.

    b.   elaborate, secret, and often wildly emotional, rituals.

    c.   sophisticated theologies combining revealed truths with philosophical rationalization.

    d.   promise of an afterlife to compensate for the rigors of life in the world.

GUIDE TO DOCUMENTS

I. Oedipus' Self-Mutilation

1. What, for the Greeks, might be the primary lesson to be learned from this tragedy?

    a.   Life is cruel.

    b.   Sin requires atonement.

    c.   If a man destroys the eye of another, his eye shall be destroyed.

    d.   Happiness is inevitably followed by sorrow.

2. What psychological insights are revealed in this excerpt?

II. Thucydides: The Melian Dialogue

1. The attitude of the Athenian speaker can best be characterized as

    a. vengeful.

    b. remorseless.

    c. sadistic.

    d. hypocritical.

2. Put into your own words, first, the argument of the Athenians and, second, the argument of the Melians. Which do you find more compelling? Why?

III. Socrates Is Sentenced to Death

1. What was Socrates' attitude toward the jury and Athenians?

    a. Forgiving.

    b. Bitter.

    c. Loving.

    d. Sarcastic.

2. According to Socrates, what were the qualities of "the good man"?

IV. The Training of a Wife

1. The responsibilities of the wife in the selection included all of the following EXCEPT

    a. superintending all the servants.

    b. managing the household's money.

    c. arranging the production of clothing

    d. rewarding and punishing members of the household

2. The author of the textbook characterizes "the education of a young wife" as "like the training of a young animal." Does this passage support that characterization? Explain the reasons for your answer.

SIGNIFICANT INDIVIDUALS

1. Aeschylus (ES-ki-lus)

2. Sophocles (SOF-ō-klēz)

3. Euripides (u-RIP-i-dēz)

4. Aristophanes (ar-is-TOF-a-nēz)

5. Herodotus (he-ROD-ō-tus)

6. Thucydides (thū-SID-i-dēz)

7. Thales of Miletus
   (THĀ-lēz of me-LĒ-tus)

8. Pythagoras of Samos
   (pi-THAG-ō-ras)

9. Democritus of Abdera
   (de-MOK-ri-tus)

10. Socrates

11. Plato

12. Aristotle

13. Zeno

14. Epicurus

15. Philip II

16. Alexander the Great

17. Darius III

18. Aristarchus (ar-is-TAR-kus)

19. Eratosthenes
    (er-a-TOS-tha-nēz)

20. Ptolemy of Alexandria
    (TOL-e-mi)

21. Euclid (Ū-klid)

22. Archimedes

a. Author of the *Oresteia* trilogy of plays (525?-456)

b. Founder of the Stoic school of philosophy (333?-262)

c. Philosopher who focused on the study of nature (384-322)

d. The greatest mathematician of antiquity (287?-212)

e. Historian of the Peloponnesian Wars (455?-399?)

f. Astronomer who championed the heliocentric theory of the universe (190?-after 126)

g. Early philosopher who taught that everything is made of water (625-ca. 546)

h. King of Macedonia who established dominance over most of Greece (359-336)

i. Astronomer whose geocentric model of the universe was accepted for over 1500 years (ca. 140 A.D.)

j. Philosopher who redirected philosophy from natural to moral issues (469-399)

k. King of Persia defeated by Alexander the Great (336-330)

l. Author of *Medea* and other tragedies (480?-406?)

m. Historian of the Persian Wars (484?-425?)

n. Satiric playwright (448?-385?)

o. Geometer whose theorems are still taught (ca. 300)

p. Philosopher who wrote the *Republic* (428-347)

q. Philosopher who focused on mathematics (ca. 530)

r. King of Macedonia who conquered Persia (336-323)

s. Author of the plays *Oedipus Rex* and *Antigone* (496?-406)

t. Astronomer who calculated the earth's circumference (275?-194?)

u. Philosopher who strove for tranquillity (341-270)

v. Philosopher who helped originate atomic theory (ca. 450)

CHRONOLOGICAL DIAGRAM

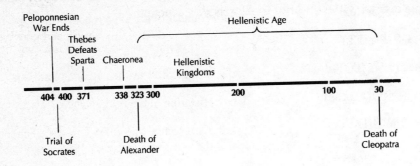

IDENTIFICATION

1. Hellenistic

2. Chaeronea (ker-o-NĒ-a)

3. Alexandria

4. Gaugamela (GO-guh-mĕ-luh)

5. Hellenization

6. *koiné*

7. Selucid kingdom (si-LOO-sid)

8. Ptolemic kingdom (TOL-e-mā-ik)

a. Battle in which Alexander the Great defeated Persia

b. "Common" Greek used throughout the Hellenistic world

c. Successor state to Alexander's empire based on Egypt

d. Greek-dominated civilization after Alexander

e. Battle in which Phillip II defeated the Greek city-states

f. Great Egyptian city that was long a center of learning

g. Process of diffusion of Greek culture in the Near East

h. Largest of the successor states to Alexander's empire

MAP EXERCISES

1.   Indicate the areas controlled by Rome, Carthage, Egypt, Persia, the Greek city-states, and Macedonia around 340 B.C., prior to Alexander's conquests.

2.   Indicate which of these civilizations is a rising power during this period and which is a declining power.

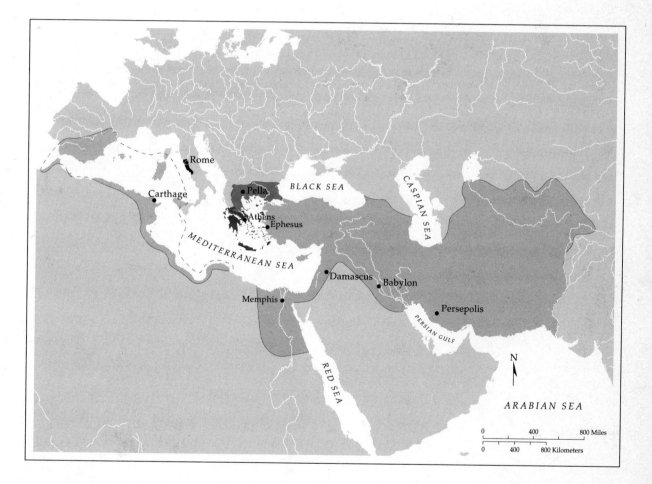

1. This map shows the Hellenistic world after Alexander's death. What does this reveal about the ability of Alexander's successors to hold his conquests together? What might this reveal about the mixing of cultures in this part of the world during the two centuries following Alexander's death?

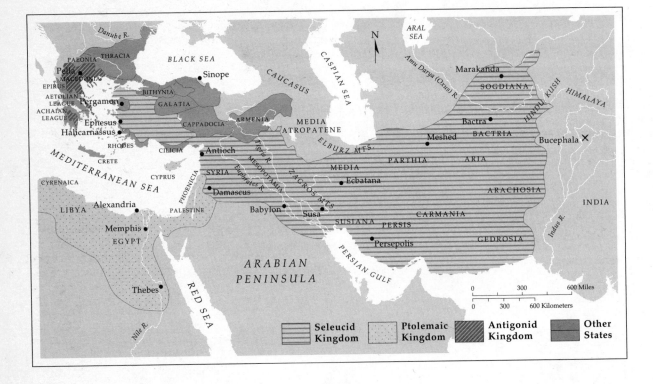

PROBLEMS FOR ANALYSIS

I. Classical Greek Culture

1. In what ways does Greek drama reflect characteristics of Greek culture as well as universal human problems?

2. Trace the evolution of Greek philosophy from its beginnings in the seventh century B.C. to Aristotle in the fourth century B.C. What historical trends in Athenian life does this evolution reflect?

3. Analyze the position of women in Greek society.

II. The Rise of Macedonia

1. "The Macedonian conquest of Greece was really a blessing in disguise." Do you agree? Explain.

III. The Hellenistic Age

1. Compare the Classical Age with the Hellenistic Age. What are the main differences?

2. How did the spread of Greeks into the East affect those areas? What were the economic and cultural consequences of Hellenization?

3. Some people argue that literature, art, science, and philosophy did not decline after the fourth century, but that they simply turned to other styles and concerns equal in quality to those of the earlier period. Do you agree?

SPECULATIONS

1. How does the civilization of fifth-and fourth-century Athens compare with our own? In which would you rather live? Why?

2. "Whether or not Alexander had high ideals behind his conquests, he and his followers should be praised, for they infused relatively backward civilizations with more advanced Greek institutions and ideals." Do you agree? Why?

3. "It is a mistake to be so admiring of the ancient Greeks. We think highly of their civilization only because it resembles our own in some ways, and we overlook the fact that it was based upon slave labor, the subjection of women, and almost perpetual warfare." Do you agree? Why?

TRANSITIONS

In "The Forming of Greek Civilization," the evolution of Greek civilization from Minoan and Mycenaean origins to the fifth-century war between Athens and Sparta was traced.

In "Classical and Hellenistic Greece," intellectual and artistic achievements of Classical Greece and the succeeding Hellenistic Age are examined. Politically, however, the Greek city-states declined. Philip II and Alexander the Great of Macedonia were able to conquer the Greeks. The victories of Alexander in the East led to the formation of powerful warring Hellenistic kingdoms, relative prosperity, and an expansion of Greek culture.

In "The Roman Republic," the development of Roman civilization through the first century B.C. will be traced. During this period political dominance over the Mediterranean will shift westward, the Romans ultimately conquering the various parts of the Hellenistic world while absorbing aspects of its culture.

ANSWERS

Self Test

1b; 2b; 3a; 4d; 5d; 6b; 7a; 8c; 9a; 10c; 11d; 12c; 13d; 14a; 15d; 16b; 17b; 18b; 19c; 20c

Guide to Documents

I-1b; II-1b; III-1a; IV-1a

Significant Individuals

1a; 2s; 3l; 4n; 5m; 6e; 7g; 8q; 9v; 10j; 11p; 12c; 13b; 14u; 15h; 16r; 17k; 18f; 19t; 20i; 21o; 22d

Identification

1d; 2e; 3f; 4a; 5g; 6b; 7h; 8c

FOUR
THE ROMAN REPUBLIC

CHAPTER HIGHLIGHTS

1. Through a number of long wars, a series of internal struggles, and a system of confederation, the Romans unified the Italian peninsula under their rule. Plebeians struggled with the long-dominant patricians for political power.

2. Wars and interventions in Africa, Spain, Greece, and Asia Minor made Rome the supreme Mediterranean power.

3. In their religion and culture, Romans were heavily influenced by the Greeks, but they developed their own rites and literature.

4. Between 133 and 31, Rome experienced a slow revolution marked by the rise of powerful men, such as Sulla, Pompey, and Julius Caesar, resulting in the fall of the Republic.

5. Octavian defeated his competitors, brought the Republic to an end, and established the structures of the Empire.

CHAPTER OUTLINE

I. The Unification of Italy (to 264 B.C.)

1. The Geography of Italy

2. Early Rome

3. The Struggle of the Orders (494–287 B.C.)

4. Roman Society in the Republic

5. Early Expansion of Rome

II. The Age of Mediterranean Conquest (264–133 B.C.)

1. The Punic Wars

2. Expansion in the Eastern Mediterranean

3. The Nature of Roman Expansion

III. The Roman Revolution (133–27 B.C.)

1. Social Change and the Gracchi

2. The Years of the Warlords

3. The First Triumvirate

4. The Supremacy of Julius Caesar

IV. The End of the Roman Republic

1. The Second Triumvirate

2. Octavian Triumphant

V. The Founding of the Roman Empire

1. Augustus and the Principate

2. Augustus, the First Roman Emperor

SELF TEST

1. Italy's geography is characterized by all of the following EXCEPT

    a. the peninsula is bisected by the Apennine mountain range.

    b. the mountains divide the land into many small valleys.

    c. in the north, the Po River runs through a large, fertile valley.

    d. the mountains are so gentle that they can be used for pasturing.

2. After throwing off Etruscan rule around 500 B.C., Roman government included all of the following EXCEPT

    a. two consuls, elected annually.

    b. a Senate consisting of men who had held elected office.

    c. three assemblies that included all adult male citizens.

    d. a dictator, whose term of office was limited to one year.

3. The outcome of the "Struggle of the Orders" between 494 and 287 B.C. was

    a. the patrician class was able to stifle all attempts at reform by assassinating plebeian leaders.

    b. the plebeians destroyed patrician dominance and installed direct control of the government by the masses.

    c. the patricians made significant concessions that did not fundamentally compromise their dominance.

    d. the plebeians wrested control of the state, but left the patricians significant ceremonial functions.

4. Women's' status in Republican Rome changed in which of the following ways?

    a. Originally subordinate to a rigid patriarchy, they gradually won significant, if still limited, freedoms.

    b. Originally relatively autonomous, they found themselves subjected to increasing patriarchal controls.

    c. Originally subordinate to a rigid patriarchy, they eventually won extensive political and civil rights.

    d. Originally relatively autonomous, they successfully maintained their position as Roman society changed.

5. Roman expansion in Italy was characterized by

    a. brutal disregard for the rights of the conquered people.

    b. an unbroken series of successful campaigns of conquest.

    c. integration of conquered states into the Roman federation.

    d. reliance on diplomacy rather than military conquest.

6. The outcome of the Punic Wars was

    a. Rome and Carthage divided control of the Western Mediterranean.

    b. Rome took the Western Mediterranean while Carthage retained the Eastern half.

    c. Rome destroyed Carthage and took control of the Western Mediterranean.

    d. Rome turned to conquest in the Eastern Mediterranean when it was unable to defeat Carthage

7. The Roman conquest of the Eastern Mediterranean

   a. occurred piecemeal as one conquest generated conflicts that led to further conquests.

   b. occurred in one fell swoop when Rome defeated the Hellenistic Kingdom at Magnesia.

   c. spared Greece, whose independent culture the Romans held in particularly high regard.

   d. led to political reforms in the conquered states that ended their chronic corruption.

8. Roman conquest of the Mediterranean was based on all of the following EXCEPT

   a. the military weakness of its enemies.

   b. a corrupt but efficient system of taxation.

   c. absolute rule of overseas provinces by Roman governors.

   d. a powerful and resilient military machine.

9. The poverty that led to the Gracchi brothers' reform efforts resulted from all of the following EXCEPT

   a. the wars with Carthage had ravaged the countryside and brought he farmers to financial ruin.

   b. citizens who profited from the wars bought out the farmers, forcing them to become landless laborers.

   c. slaves captured in the wars of conquest undercut the wage structure for free workers.

   d. the requirement that men buy their own arms and armor, which limited opportunities in the legions.

10. Gaius Marius redirected the loyalty of the Roman soldiers from the state to their generals by

   a. opening recruitment to propertyless men and securing booty and land for them.

   b. tightening recruitment to only men of property and suppressing the Italian rebellion.

   c. enlisting masses of slaves who had no roots in Rome and no prospects beyond the success of their patron.

   d. leading them on campaigns of conquest that made each of them master of numerous foreign slaves.

11. Lucius Cornelius Sulla did all of the following EXCEPT

   a. lead an army into Rome for the first time to secure political power.

   b. make himself dictator without the usual six month time limit.

   c. enact conservative reforms increasing the power of the Senate.

   d. abolish the minimum ages at which a man could hold offices.

12. Pompey accomplished all of the following EXCEPT

   a. he had himself elected as the first dictator for life.

   b. he established a system of client kings in smaller states.

   c. he reversed many of the reforms enacted by Sulla.

   d. he suppressed piracy and resettled many pirates onto farms.

13. Julius Caesar extended Rome's control over

   a. Spain.

   b. Syria.

   c. Gaul.

   d. Germany.

14. To secure his power, Julius Caesar did all of the following EXCEPT

    a. style himself as champion of the people.

    b. lead an army on Rome.

    c. make himself dictator for life.

    d. ruthlessly persecute his enemies.

15. Julius Caesar was killed by

    a. aristocrats, who resented his usurpation of their traditional dominance of the state.

    b. plebeians, who wanted revenge for his ruthless suppression of popular rights.

    c. rival generals, who hoped to gain his power for themselves.

    d. his officers, who felt he had neglected them after they helped him gain power.

16. The Second Triumvirate included all of the following EXCEPT

    a. Mark Antony.

    b. Octavian.

    c. Brutus.

    d. Marcus Lepidus.

17. Octavian ultimately won control over Rome by

    a. humbling the Senate.

    b. defeating Antony and Cleopatra.

    c. taking control of each province in turn.

    d. reorganizing the armies to include non-Romans.

18. Octavian secured his control over Rome by all of the following EXCEPT

    a. restoring the Republic while dominating it behind the scenes.

    b. gaining the powers and populist stature of a tribune.

    c. securing command of the all of the armies.

    d. creating the powerful office of "Augustus." for himself.

19. During his reign, Augustus accomplished all of the following EXCEPT

    a. ending the series of civil wars.

    b. establishing secure borders.

    c. deifying the office of emperor.

    d. advancing the rights of women.

GUIDE TO DOCUMENTS

The Murder of Julius Caesar

1. In this account of the murder of Julius Caesar, what impression is the author, Plutarch, trying to create in the minds of readers?

    a. That Pompey was responsible for Caesar's murder.

    b. That Brutus' betrayal crushed Caesar's spirit.

    c. That Caesar deserved the fate that befell him.

    d. That the entire Senate supported the conspirators.

2. What does this reveal about the problems facing the Senate in these last years of the Roman Republic?

SIGNIFICANT INDIVIDUALS

1. Hannibal

2. Polybius (po-LIB-i-us)

3. Tiberius Gracchus (GRAK-us)

4. Marius

5. Sulla

6. Pompey (POM-pi)

7. Julius Caesar

8. Cicero

9. Mark Antony

10. Lucretius (lu-KRĒ-shi-us)

11. Octavian (Augustus)

12. Cleopatra

a. Founder of the Roman Empire (63 B.C.-14 A.D.)

b. General and consul who lost to Julius Caesar (106-48)

c. General and consul who made himself dictator for life (100-44)

d. Carthaginian general (247-183)

e. Conservative politician and writer (106-43)

f. Tribune who attempted land redistribution (162-133)

g. Last queen of Egypt (51-49, 48-30)

h. Latin poet (94-55)

i. Roman general who reformed the army (157-86)

j. Protégé of Caesar and consort of Cleopatra (83?-30)

k. Conservative general and dictator (138-78)

l. Greek historian (200?-118?)

CHRONOLOGICAL DIAGRAM

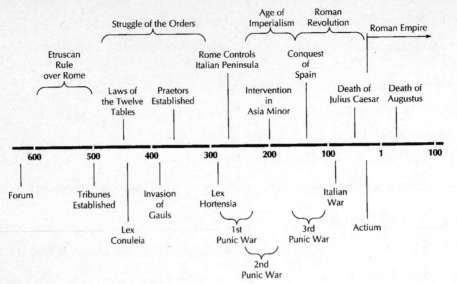

IDENTIFICATION

1. Consul

2. Senate

3. Struggle of the Orders

4. Tribune

5. *Lex Canuleia*

6. Equestrians

7. Italian War

8. Tribal Assembly

9. Amicitia (am-ī-SIT-i-a)

10. First Triumvirate

11. Actium

12. *Lex Hortensia*

a. Revolt over citizenship rights

b. Representative of the plebeians

c. One of two executives with *imperium*

d. Alliance between Caesar, Pompey, and Crassius

e. The conservative nerve center of the state

f. The battle at which Octavian won final control of Rome

g. Rome's informal arrangement with minor client kings

h. Law making Tribal Assembly's decisions binding on state

i. Wealthy class of businessmen

j. Process by which plebeians won greater political rights

k. Law permitting plebeians and patricians to marry

l. Residentially based popular council

MAP EXERCISES

1. Label the main political powers of the Mediterranean basin around 264 B.C.

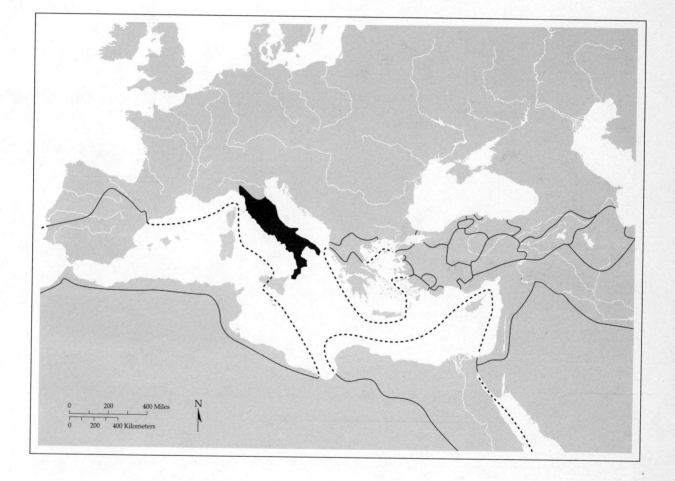

1. Indicate the main areas and dates of Roman expansion between 264 and 44 B.C. Compare this map and the previous map. At whose expense did Rome expand during this period?

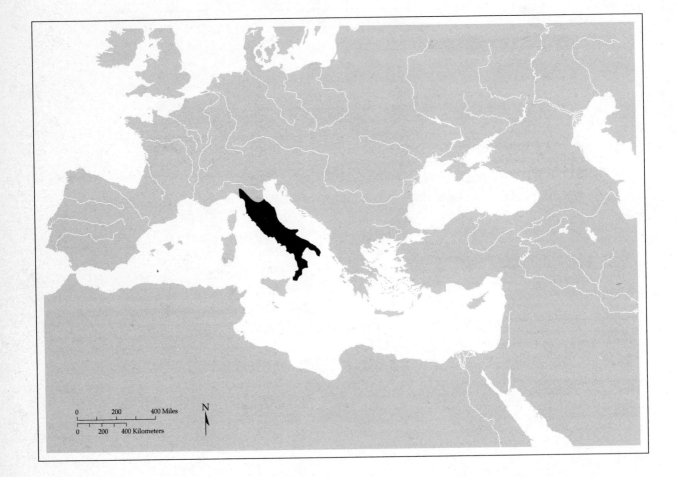

PROBLEMS FOR ANALYSIS

I. The Unification of Italy

1. Polybius called the Roman constitution a perfect blend of regal, aristocratic, and democratic elements. Do you agree? Explain.

2. How were the Romans able to hold their growing territories together during the early period of the Roman Republic?

3. What was the nature of Roman society, religion, and culture? What connections might be drawn between the three?

II. The Age of Mediterranean Conquest

1. Trace the main steps by which Rome became an imperial power. What role did Rome's system of alliances and its method of provincial administration play in this?

III. The Roman Revolution

1. What were the fundamental strains and changes that undermined the foundations of the Roman Republic? How is this reflected in the developments concerning Tiberius and Gaius Gracchus?

2. What role did powerful generals play in the decline of the Republic? Use examples.

3. How did the Senate respond to threats? Did it simply give up, respond in kind, or pursue policies that further undermined its own authority?

IV. The End of the Roman Republic

1. How was Octavian able to acquire supreme power over his competitors?

2. In what ways did Octavian's victory mark the end of the Roman Republic and the Hellenistic Age?

V. The Founding of the Roman Empire

1. What policies did Augustus follow to secure his own power and establish the structure of the Roman Empire?

SPECULATIONS

1. Suppose you were a Roman. Present arguments justifying Roman expansion as something more than ruthless territorial acquisition.

2. What policies should the Senate have followed to prevent the fall of the Roman Republic? Do you think it would have been better if the Republic had been preserved? Explain.

3. Compare the strengths and weaknesses of the Greeks and Romans.

TRANSITIONS

In "Classical and Hellenistic Greece," Greek civilization at its height as well as its spread and transformation in the East under Alexander and his successors were examined.

In "The Roman Republic," the Romans—driven by a desire to impose themselves on all others, supported by large reserves of manpower, and aided by an authoritarian view of life—succeeded in unifying most of the Mediterranean and European worlds under their rule. In the latter years of the Republic a revolution eliminated political freedom. Years of instability were finally brought to an end by Octavian, who effectively established the Roman Empire.

In "The Empire and Christianity," the Roman Empire as its height, the growth of a new religion (Christianity), and the transformation and decline of the Empire will be examined.

ANSWERS

Self Test

1b; 2d; 3c; 4a; 5c; 6c; 7a; 8a; 9d; 10a; 11d; 12a; 13c; 14d; 15a; 16c; 17b; 18d; 19c

Guide to Documents

1b

Significant Individuals

1d; 2l; 3f; 4i; 5k; 6b; 7c; 8e; 9j; 10h; 11a; 12g

Identification

1c; 2e; 3j; 4b; 5k; 6i; 7a; 8l; 9g; 10d; 11f; 12h

CHAPTER HIGHLIGHTS

1. Thanks to an effective government, a well-functioning corps of civil servants, and a generally reliable defense force, the two centuries after the death of Augustus were a period of relative peace, prosperity, and creative accomplishment.

2. In the third century the Empire experienced political instability, economic decline, social turmoil, and cultural disintegration.

3. Although reforms by Diocletian and Constantine extended the life of the Empire, the Western Empire succumbed to a number of problems and fell—marking a turning point in history.

4. Despite initial opposition from the government and from heretical divisions, the Christian Church formulated dogma and eventually became the Empire's official religion.. Christianity's rise and triumph amounted to a cultural revolution in the Classical world.

CHAPTER OUTLINE

I. The Empire at Its Height

1. The Successors of Augustus

2. The Five Good Emperors

3. Roman Imperial Civilization

II. Changes in Ancient Society

1. The Period of Crisis (192–284)

2. Cultural Disintegration

III. The Late Roman Empire

1. Restoration under Diocletian

2. Constantine and the Bureaucracy

3. The Decline of the Western Empire

IV. Christianity and Its Early Rivals

1. The Mystery Religions

2. The Jews in the Roman Empire

3. Origins of Christianity

4. Battles within Christianity

5. The Fathers of the Church

SELF TEST

1. Which of the following was NOT one of he three unifying elements that held together the Roman Empire?

    a. The figure of the emperor.

    b. The civil bureaucracy.

    c. The army.

    d. The priesthood.

2. None of the Julio-Claudian emperors after Augustus were particularly distinguished, but they managed to

    a. add extensive territories in the East.

    b. preserve the empire in peace.

    c. recast provincial administration.

    d. restore power to the Senate.

3. A key to stability during the reign of the "Five Good Emperors" was their practice of

    a. involving the Praetorian Guard in the process of picking a successor.

    b. insisting that the eldest son should succeed an emperor upon his death.

    c. allowing the Senate to elect their successor before their death.

    d. adopting a well qualified leader as their son and successor.

4. During the late Republic and early Empire, the economy was characterized by all of the following EXCEPT

    a. extraordinary prosperity.

    b. the growth of towns in the West to rival those of the East.

    c. the growth of commercial estates in place of small farms in Italy.

    d. the growth of provincial areas in competition with Italy.

5. All of the following characterized society in the first centuries of the Roman Empire EXCEPT

    a. exceptionally high living standards for the upper classes.

    b. conditions for the urban workers far below those of the peasantry.

    c. considerable social mobility.

    d. a huge population dependent on public allotments of grain.

6. Permanent Roman contributions to Western Civilization included all of the following EXCEPT

    a. a rich and complex system of civil law.

    b. the extension of literature to the lower classes.

    c. the use of arches and vault on a large scale.

    d. a system of roads across Western Europe.

7. All of the following contributed to the period of crisis from 192 to 284 EXCEPT

    a. economic decline.

    b. debilitating wars along the frontiers.

    c. the rise of Christianity.

    d. the decline of efficient administration.

8. Which of the following did the Roman slave system accomplish?

    a. It provided a reliable work force with strong incentives to work hard.

    b. It promoted technological innovation to replace human power with machinery.

    c. It permitted a calculated use of labor in relation to land and capital.

    d. It insured a reliable flow of replacement workers for the aging and the dead.

9. The government tried to reverse rural depopulation by all of the following EXCEPT

    a. allowing foreigners to settle on unused land within the Empire.

    b. attracting free Romans from the cities by offering land on good terms.

    c. freeing large numbers of slaves and granting them farmsteads.

    d. prohibiting farmers and their children from leaving their farm.

10. The chief weakness of Classical culture was that it

    a. had always lacked intellectual sophistication.

    b. appealed mainly to the privileged.

    c. maintained an optimism that rang increasingly false.

    d. became increasingly corrupted by popular elements.

11. Diocletian restored the stability of the Empire by doing all of the following EXCEPT

    a. converting to Christianity.

    b. sharing power with three other rulers.

    c. establishing an authoritarian bureaucracy.

    d. strengthening the tax system.

12. By the end of Constantine's rule, all of the following were true EXCEPT

    a. the capital had been moved to Byzantium, which came to be known as Constantinople.

    b. the Roman army had ceased to be an effective force, since repeated defeats demoralized it.

    c. the economy had become virtually stagnant, as the state tried to force people to produce.

    d. government had become remote from the people, with the emperor insulated even from the court.

13. All of the following are reasons given for the fall of the Western Empire EXCEPT

    a. economic decline caused by the decline of trade and a labor shortage.

    b. social decay caused by governmental regulation of productive people and support of unproductive ones.

    c. cultural disillusionment as Romans satisfied with traditional religion rejected official Christianity.

    d. geographic conditions that made it easier for invaders to move into the West than the East.

14. Christianity differed from all of the mystery religions because it

    a. held out the promise of a blessed afterlife.

    b. held its teachings to be a greater mystery than theirs.

    c. involved initiation rites leading to an ecstatic experience of God.

    d. called on its adherence to practice love and justice in their daily lives.

15. The Jewish factions included all of the following EXCEPT

    a. the Sadducees, formed of the landed aristocracy and the high priests.

    b. the Pharisees, who were pious middle-class lay people.

    c. the Essenes, ascetic priests who settled at Qumran.

    d. the Eleusians, poor farmers awaiting the Messiah.

16. St. Paul's critical contribution to Christianity was

    a. to end Jewish participation in the persecution of Christians.

    b. to convert his fellow Pharisee to Christianity.

    c. to show that Christianity was a direct continuation of Jewish traditions.

    d. to open the religion to Gentiles as well as Jews.

17. The development of Church government was characterized by all of the following EXCEPT

    a. the gradual exclusion of women.

    b. the steady strengthening of the power of bishops.

    c. creation of a resilient institutional structure.

    d. increasing exclusiveness towards potential converts.

18. The adoption of Christianity as the Empire's official religion resulted in

    a. the use of government repression against the Church's opponents.

    b. the end to all persecution of religions by the government.

    c. a civil war between adherents of the old religion and the new.

    d. the rapid collapse of the Western Empire.

19. The chief value of heresies to Christianity was that they

    a. created alternative forms of the religion that helped it appeal to a broad range of people.

    b. forced it to define its doctrines ever more clearly.

    c. drew off people whose lacked a genuine commitment to the religion.

    d. encouraged Christians to practice love and tolerance toward each other.

20. The relationship between Christianity and pagan Classical culture was that

    a. Christians rejected any attempt to make use of pagan texts.

    b. Classical paganism gradually eroded belief in Christian revelation.

    c. pagans refused to allow Christians to utilize their educational materials.

    d. Christians used pagan texts as educational tools, thereby preserving them.

21. The Church fathers were important for all of the following reasons EXCEPT

    a. they produced commentaries and histories that were models for future generations.

    b. they refined the text of the Scriptures in light of the original Hebrew and translated them into Latin.

    c. they accommodated the teachings of Christian morality to peoples' natural urges for sex and comfort.

    d. they established the doctrine that the church was in spiritual matters above the government.

GUIDE TO DOCUMENTS

I. Tacitus on the Powers of Augustus

1. Tacitus explains Augustus' acquisition of supreme power by all of the following EXCEPT

    a. his liberal use of bribery.

    b. the rapidity with which he seized power.

    c. people's happiness with the peace and order he created.

    d. the fact that all other strong men had been killed.

2. What does this reveal about the state of government prior to this acquisition of power by Augustus?

II. Augustine Is Brought to His Faith

1. According to this excerpt Augustine converted because

    a. he realized that it had taken a child to show him the truth.

    b. he realized that he was being foolish to wait upon a sign from God.

    c. he had tired of his worldly ways and lost his desire to indulge himself.

    d. the incident convinced him that God had heard and answered his prayers.

2. How does this conversion relate to some of the later doctrines favored by Augustine, such as those related to sex and renunciation?

3. How might this explain some of the appeal of Christianity?

SIGNIFICANT INDIVIDUALS

1. Virgil

2. Horace

3. Augustus

4. Livy

5. Tacitus (TAS-e-tes)

6. Paul

7. Felicitas (FĒ-lĭ-sit-ās)

8. Diocletian (dī-e-KLĒ-shen)

9. Constantine

10. Ambrose of Milan

11. Jerome

12. Augustine of Hippo

a. Last and greatest of the Church fathers (354-430)

b. Translator of the Bible into Latin (340?-420)

c. Bishop who excommunicated Theodosius (340?-397)

d. Servant martyred with her mistress (ca. 203)

e. Author of the *Aeneid* (70-19)

f. First Roman emperor (27 B.C.-14 A.D.)

g. First Roman emperor to convert to Christianity (306-337)

h. Poet who wrote *Odes, Epodes* and *Satires* (65-8)

i. Leading Roman historian (55?-120?)

j. Historian who celebrated rise of Rome (59 B.C.-17 A.D.)

k. Emperor who restored 3rd century empire (284-305)

l. Missionary and author of epistles (1st Century A.D.)

CHRONOLOGICAL DIAGRAM

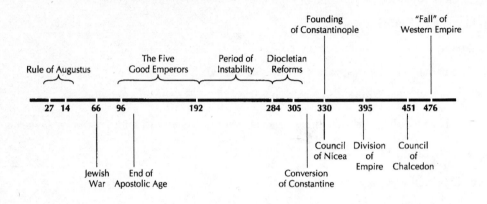

IDENTIFICATION

1. *Latifundia* (lat-e-FUN-dē-e)

2. "Bread and Circuses"

3. jurists

4. *Ius civile* (i-ūs sī-vī-le)

5. aqueduct

6. Pompeii (pom-PĂ-ē)

7. *coloni* (kol-ō-ni)

8. Mithraism (MITH-ra-ism)

9. Essenes (ES-ēn)

10. The Great Persecutions

11. Milvian Bridge

12. Donatists

13. Nicene Creed (NĪ-sēn)

14. *The City of God*

15. Tetrarchy

a. Concerted attempt by Diocletan to suppress Christianity

b. Competitor to Christianity popular among soldiers

c. Heretics who refused sacraments from *traditores*

d. Great commercial agricultural estates worked by slaves

e. Book contrasting spiritual and worldly communities

f. Roman system of civil law

g. Member of Jewish sect awaiting savior

h. Citizens familiar with the law who advised judges

i. Tenant farmer

j. Co-rule by four emperors instituted by Diocletian

k. Town buried and thereby preserved by volcanic eruption

l. Battle that led Constantine to convert to Christianity

m. Policy of buying off the unemployed masses

n. Huge structures used to channel water to cities

o. Anti-Arian doctrine asserting Christ's equality to God

MAP EXERCISES

1. Indicate the outlines of the Empire in 14 A.D. and its subsequent maximum expansion.

2. Indicate the geographic expansion of Christianity around the year 312.

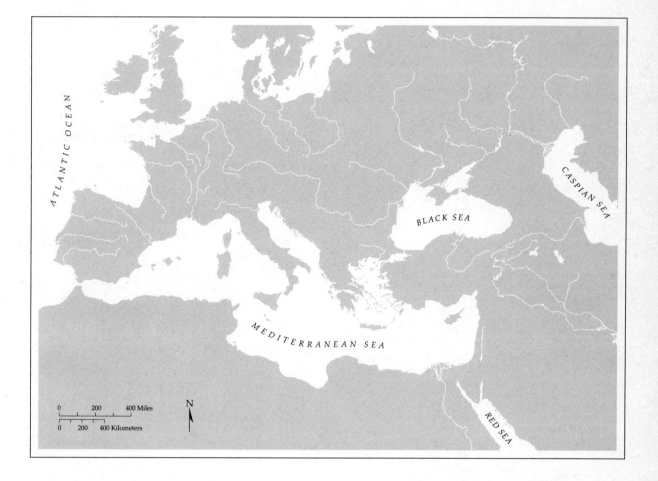

1. During the fourth century the Roman Empire was divided into Western and Eastern halves. Considering that many of the invaders came from the north and northeast, what geographical factors help explain the vulnerability of the West compared to that of the East?

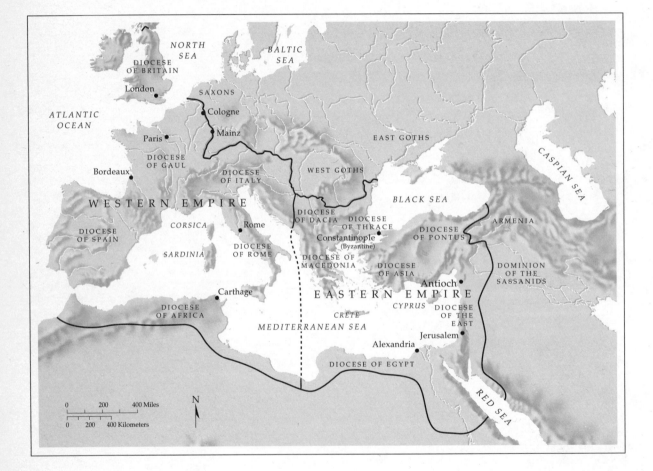

PROBLEMS FOR ANALYSIS

I. The Empire at Its Height

1. Analyze the way in which the socioeconomic system of the Empire functioned. What were its economic characteristics? What were the major social classes? How well did it function?

2. Historians argue that Romans were most skilled in law, engineering, and architecture. Using examples, support this argument.

II. Changes in Ancient Society

1. While in the short run slavery as an economic system worked well, in the long run it worked to the disadvantage of the Empire. Explain.

2. Analyze the crisis of the third century. How is this reflected in the cultural disintegration of the period?

III. The Late Roman Empire

1. What problems did the reforms of Diocletian and Constantine solve, and what new problems did they create?

2. Assess the different interpretations of the Roman Empire in the West. Which one, or which combination, seem most persuasive?

IV. Christianity and Its Early Rivals

1. Analyze the similarities and differences of Christianity and other mystery religions. What characteristics of Christianity contributed to its success?

2. How did women's role in Christianity change over time? What accounts for the change?

3. How did theological controversies contribute to establishing Christian dogma and order within the Church?

SPECULATIONS

1. As an early leader of the Christian Church, what policies should you follow to ensure the spread of a single Christian religion? Why?

2. What might Roman emperors have done to prevent the fall of the Empire in the West?

3. Hold a debate between representatives of a pagan Classical culture and a Christian culture. Indicate the main points and responses each would make.

TRANSITIONS

In "The Roman Republic," the rise of Rome as a world power was traced. The period ended with the fall of the Republic and the establishment of the Empire by Augustus.

In "The Empire and Christianity," the story begins with the period just after the establishment of the Empire by Augustus. For about two centuries the Empire prospered, but during the third century a long series of crises occurred. Several dynamic emperors restored the situation in the fourth century, but gradually the Empire split, and the Western half collapsed in the fifth century. Numerous factors— including flaws in the slave economy, conflicting values, and changes in all sectors of life—weakened the Empire, causing it to decline. Yet at the same time people were laying the basis for a new civilization, above all by building on the legacy of Rome and spreading a new set of religious beliefs—Christianity.

In "The Making of Western Europe," the development of a new civilization in the West between the fifth and ninth centuries will be traced.

CHRONOLOGICAL DIAGRAMS

Diagram 1
The Ancient Civilizations

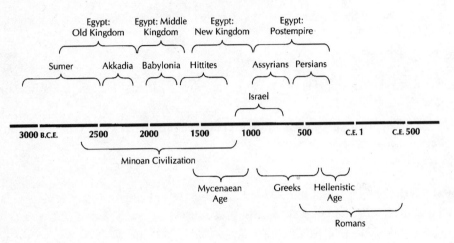

Diagram 2
Greco-Roman Civilization

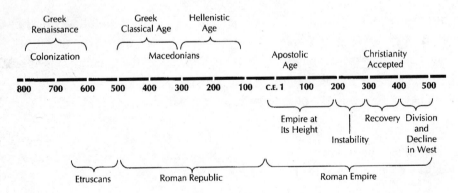

MAP EXERCISES

1.　Identify the centers and the approximate boundaries of the following civilizations:

　　a.　Babylonia, 1900 B.C.

　　b.　Egypt, 1300 B.C.

　　c.　Israel, 900 B.C.

　　d.　Persia, 500 B.C.

　　e.　Minoan and Mycenaean, 1400 B.C.

　　f.　Greece, 400 B.C.

　　g.　Hellenistic Kingdoms, 250 B.C.

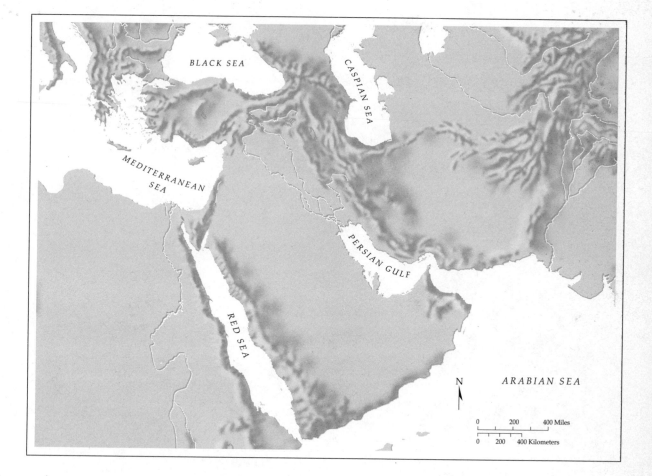

1. Identify the centers and approximate boundaries of the following:

    a. Rome, 250 B.C.

    b. Rome, 50 B.C.

    c. Rome, 150 A.D.

    d. The Eastern and Western Roman Empires, fourth century.

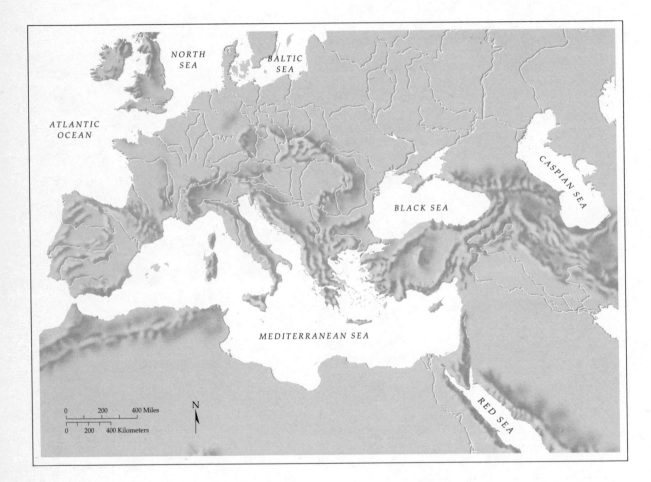

BOX CHART

Reproduce the Box Chart in a larger format in your notebook or on a separate sheet of paper. It is suggested that you devote one page for each column (i.e., chart all seven themes for each civilization on a separate page).

For a fuller explanation of the themes and how best to find material, see Introduction.

Civilization Themes	Mesopotamia Near East	Egypt	Classical Greece	Hellenistic World	Roman Republic	Roman Empire
Social Structure: Groups in Society						
Politics: Events and Structures						
Economics: Production and Distribution						
Family Gender Roles Daily Life						
War: Relationship to larger society						
Religion: Beliefs, Communities, Conflicts						
Cultural Expression: Formal and Popular						

CULTURAL STYLES

1. Compare the sculpture shown on pages 8 and the relief shown on page 18. In what ways do these convey differences between Mesopotamian and Egyptian civilization?

2. Compare the sculptures shown on pages 8, 54, 81, and 84. What do the first two suggest about the relationship of early Greek culture to the older civilizations to the East? What do the latter two show about the development of Greek art and culture?

3. Compare the sculptures shown on pages 68 and 93. How did the Hellenistic era carry forward the artistic traditions of the Classical period? In what ways did it change them?

4. Compare the sculptures shown on pages 68 and 93 with those on pages 98, 106, and 117? What do they show about the relationship between Greek and Roman culture?

5. Compare the sculptures shown on pages 130 and 159. What about them is different? What about them is similar? What do these similarities and differences show about the development of the Roman empire?

ANSWERS

Self Test

1d; 2b; 3d; 4b; 5b; 6b; 7c; 8c; 9c; 10b; 11a; 12b; 13c; 14d; 15d; 16d; 17d; 18a; 19b; 20d; 21c

Guide to Documents

I-1b; II-1d

Significant Individuals

1e; 2h; 3f; 4j; 5i; 6l; 7d; 8k; 9g; 10c; 11b; 12a

Identification

1d; 2m; 3h; 4f; 5n; 6k; 7i; 8b; 9g; 10a; 11l; 12c; 13o; 14e; 15j

SIX

THE MAKING OF WESTERN EUROPE

CHAPTER HIGHLIGHTS

1. "Barbarian" peoples invaded Roman territories, merging their own institutions and culture with those of the declining Roman civilization.

2. The Eastern Roman Empire survived and evolved into the long-lasting Byzantine Empire.

3. Commerce and industry decreased, and Europe became a peasant society organized around single-family farms organized in nucleated villages on estates held by landlords.

4. The Christian Church, through the growth of the Roman papacy, monasticism, and missionary activity, maintained and spread Roman traditions of social order and Classical culture.

5. The Franks and Anglo-Saxons created kingdoms from which modern France and England would grow.

CHAPTER OUTLINE

I. The New Community of Peoples

1. The Great Migrations

2. Germanic Society

3. Germans and Romans

II. The New Political Structures

1. The Early Byzantine Empire

2. Justinian the Great

3. The Frankish Kingdom

4. Kingship in Italy and Spain

5. Anglo-Saxon England

III. The New Economy, 500–900

1. Agriculture

2. Trade and Manufacture

IV. The Expansion of the Church

1. Origins of the Papacy

2. Monasticism

3. Missionaries and Popular Religion

V. Letters and Learning

1. The Church and Classical Learning

SELF TEST

1. All of the following peoples contributed to the formation of Western Europe between the sixth and the eighth centuries EXCEPT

   a. Roman.

   b. Celtic.

   c. Kurdish.

   d. Germanic.

2. Most German tribes initially converted to which form of Christianity?

   a. Donatist.

   b. Roman.

   c. Arian.

   d. Byzantine.

3. Which Germanic tribe forged a long-lasting special relationship with the Papacy?

   a. The Franks.

   b. The Visigoths.

   c. The Ostragoths.

   d. The Lombards.

4. Germanic society was characterized by all of the following EXCEPT

   a. individual ownership of property.

   b. kindreds made up of families linked by common ancestry.

   c. chiefs, free warriors and their families, and slaves.

   d. strong kingship rooted in the distant past.

5. War influenced all of the following aspects of Germanic society EXCEPT

   a. the role of women.

   b. the importance of kings.

   c. the attitude toward children.

   d. the distribution of wealth.

6. Germanic law and procedures involved all of the following EXCEPT

   a. reliance on custom rather than written laws.

   b. councils and assemblies to advise kings and chiefs.

   c. use of sworn witnesses in judicial cases.

   d. a special role for women as judges and advisors.

7. As the Germans conquered the Western Empire, they

    a. assimilated with the existing Roman and Celtic inhabitants.

    b. exterminated the existing Roman and Celtic inhabitants.

    c. enslaved the existing Roman and Celtic inhabitants.

    d. remained separate from the existing Roman and Celtic inhabitants.

8. The Emperor Constantine transferred the capital of the Empire from West to East because

    a. the new capital was located at the intersection of two major trade routes.

    b. the East was the wealthier and more populous part of the Empire.

    c. the new capital had the aura of a Christian city.

    d. the East was less threatened by the enemies that beset the Empire.

9. The Emperor Justinian had all of the following goals EXCEPT

    a. the destruction of the Persian Empire.

    b. the reconquest of the Western provinces.

    c. the reformation of laws and institutions.

    d. the creation of splendid public works.

10. The introduction of the stirrup among the Franks had all of the following effects EXCEPT

    a. it give a final advantage to warriors fighting on horseback over warriors fighting on foot.

    b. it made warfare more expensive, fostering the creation of a specialized warrior aristocracy.

    c. it ended most freemen's importance as warriors, making them full-time peasants.

    d. it bolstered the power of the Merovingian monarchs, who gained the support of the new aristocracy.

11. The Pepin of Heristal, his son Charles Martel, and his grandson Pepin the Short usurped the Merovingian's power by doing all of the following EXCEPT

    a. distributing lands to gain the support of the new mounted warrior aristocracy.

    b. supporting the activities of Christian missionaries.

    c. defending the Pope from attacks by the Lombards in Italy.

    d. assassinating the last, feeble Merovingian king, Childeric III.

12. Early Medieval farmers adopted all of the following innovations that improved the efficiency of farming in northern European conditions EXCEPT

    a. a new set of crops including grains, wines, olive oil, and linen and woolen cloth.

    b. a new, heavy plow that turned over the soil to create furrows that drained excess water.

    c. a new harness for horses that rested on their shoulders and thus enabled them to pull a full load.

    d. a new, three-field system of crop rotation that supported two crops per year and reduced fallow.

13. Archeological evidence

    a.   confirms Pirenne's thesis that the Germanic invasions did not fundamentally alter Roman trade patterns.

    b.   confirms the older view that towns and trade collapsed because of the Germanic invasions.

    c.   has proved unable to uncover evidence to confirm or discredit Pirenne's thesis.

    d.   indicates that the Germanic invasions were neither as mild as Pirenne argued nor as destructive as traditionally thought.

14. The Bishopric of Rome grew into the Papacy because of all of the following EXCEPT

    a.   the doctrine of Petrine succession.

    b.   Rome's traditional association with central power.

    c.   the Cyprian doctrine calling the Pope the "bishop of bishops."

    d.   the Popes' role in defending and ruling central Italy.

15. The most common form of Western monasticism was known as the

    a.   Basilian.

    b.   Gregorian.

    c.   Benedictine.

    d.   Stylite.

16. Monasteries influenced Medieval society in all of the following ways EXCEPT

    a.   they set an example of good farming practices and estate management.

    b.   they provided communities independent of the structures of local power.

    c.   they preserved copies of both pagan and Christian Latin literary works.

    d.   they supplied kings with both advisors and administrators.

17. Early Medieval missionaries included all of the following EXCEPT

    a.   St. Patrick, who converted the Irish.

    b.   Gregory the Great, who converted the Angles.

    c.   Clement, who converted the Frisians.

    d.   Boniface, who converted the Bavarians.

18. An *exegeses* is

    a.   a vast, encyclopedic work.

    b.   a meditation that highlights the role of philosophy in solving human problems.

    c.   a work of commentary on and interpretation of the Bible.

    d.   a book of instructions for bishops.

GUIDE TO DOCUMENTS

I. Tacitus on the Early Germans

1. All of the following principles and practices governed the Germanic legal system EXCEPT

    a. a criminal's punishment were designed to reflect the nature of the crime.

    b. priests had a decisive influence on the assembly's deliberations.

    c. major issues required the decision of the whole community.

    d. minor issues could be decided by the chiefs alone.

2. What evidence does this provide for the nature of Germanic politics?

II. Sidonius Appolinaris on Living with the Germans

1. In Sidonius' experience, the attitude of the Germans toward the Romans was one of

    a. respect.

    b. amusement.

    c. amazement.

    d. reserve.

2. What does this passage reveal about the process by which the Roman Empire "fell?"

III. The Rule of St. Benedict on the Clothing of Monks

1. The life-style of the Benedictine monks can best be described as

    a. cozy.

    b. opulent.

    c. harsh.

    d. austere.

2. What kind of community does the passage suggest St. Benedict's rules were designed to create?

SIGNIFICANT INDIVIDUALS

1. Attila
2. Odoacer (ō-dō-A-ser)
3. Theodoric
4. Justinian
5. Theodora
6. Clovis (KLŌ-vis)
7. Charles Martel
8. Pepin the Short (PEP-in)
9. Gregory the Great
10. St. Benedict
11. Procopius (prō-KŎ-pē-us)
12. Boethius (bō-Ē-thē-us)
13. Gregory of Tours
14. Bede the Venerable (bĕd)

a. Ostrogothic king who brought peace to Italy (r. 474-526)
b. Pope who increased Papal role in world (r.590-604)
c. Byzantine empress who helped husband rule (r.527-548)
d. English scholar noted for his high standards (673?-735)
e. Frankish leader who defeated Moors at Tours (715-741)
f. Two-faced Byzantine historian (6th Century)
g. Leader of the Huns who invaded Empire(r. 433?-453)
h. Bishop who wrote *History of the Franks* (544?-594)
i. Author of *Consolation of Philosophy* (480?-524?)
j. General who deposed last Roman Emperor (r. 476-493)
k. Merovingian founder of Frankish kingdom (481-511)
l. Byzantine emperor who codified Roman Law (r.527-565)
m. Churchman who established monastic rules (480?-543?)
n. Merovingian mayor who became king (r.751-768)

CHRONOLOGICAL DIAGRAM

Early Middle Ages

Early Byzantine Period

Last Roman Emperor in West Deposed

Adrianople

Attila   Ostrogoths

Bede the Venerable

350	378	410	455	496	528	600	664	754
Huns Invade Europe		Rome sacked	Vandals Plunder Rome	Conversion of Clovis		Gregory the Great	Council of Whitby	Pepin Crowned King

Codex Justinanus

IDENTIFICATION

1. Celts
2. Huns
3. Ostrogoths
4. Visigoths
5. Franks
6. Slavs
7. *Wergeld* (VER-gelt)
8. animal style
9. Constantinople
10. Hagia Sophia (HĀ-jē-uh SŎ-fē-uh)
11. *Codex Justinianus*
12. cavalry
13. stirrup
14. heavy plow
15. tandem harness
16. three-field system
17. papal primacy
18. Benedictine rule

a. Domed church that served as model for Byzantine
b. Fighters mounted on horseback
c. Doctrine that the Pope is predominant in Christianity
d. Germanic artistic tradition influential in Medieval art
e. Systemization of Roman law still influential today
f. "Western" Goths who established kingdom in Spain
g. Farm implement facilitating cultivation of northern soils
h. Farm implement facilitating use of teams of horses
i. Inhabitants of northwestern Europe before Romans
j. Basic regulations for Western European monasteries

k. "Eastern" Goths who established kingdom in Italy
l. Crop rotation scheme that increased productivity of land
m. People who settled in eastern Europe
n. Germanic tribe that settled in and took control of Gaul
o. Foothold attached to saddle to help secure rider on horse
p. Asiatic people whose forays started Germanic migrations
q. Capital of the Late Roman and Byzantine Empire
r. Money paid as compensation for a person's life

MAP EXERCISE

1.   Indicate the areas where the Vandals, Visigoths, Franks, Anglo-Saxons, Burgundians, Alemanni, and Ostrogoths settled.

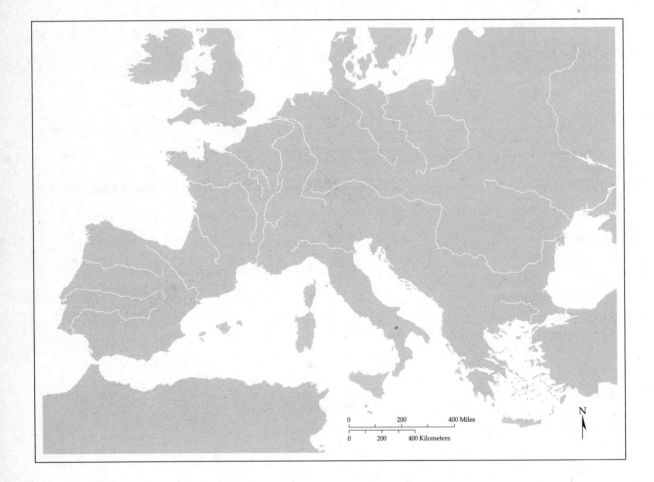

PROBLEMS FOR ANALYSIS

I. The New Community of Peoples

1. Considering the numerous invasions of the Roman Empire by Celtic, Germanic, and Slavic tribes, was there a pattern to their conquests and settlements? Explain.

2. Despite many differences between Germans and Romans, the Germans assimilated into the culture of the Roman Empire. How do you explain this?

3. What legal, political, military, and cultural institutions did the Germans bring with them? Indicate any connections between these and later medieval institutions.

II. The New Political Structures

1. Justinian was both successful and unsuccessful in carrying out his ambitious plans. Compare his accomplishments with his ambitions. Do you think he would be considered a Roman or a Byzantine emperor? Why?

2. What was the relationship between German kings and the surviving elements of the Roman Empire? Why did this relationship come about?

3. How did changes in warfare affect Frankish society? How were these social changes related to the rise of Pepin of Heristal and his descendants?

III. The New Economy

1. In what ways did Europeans make important technological and organizational changes in the economy of the Early Middle Ages?

2. What does the dispute over the decline of trade and towns in the Early Middle Ages reveal about the different sources of information that historians use?

IV. The Expansion of the Church

1. How were the early Roman bishops able to develop themselves into powerful popes? What role did Gregory the Great play in this development?

2. Why was monasticism so important? What were the characteristics of monasticism? Why was the Benedictine rule so important?

3. What peoples were converted to Christianity during this period? What groups in the Christian West supplied and supported the missionary initiative?

V. Letters and Learning

1. In what ways was Classical culture saved and transformed by the Church? Why was Classical culture so important to the Church?

SPECULATIONS

1. Suppose you were a bishop of Rome during the Early Middle Ages. What do you think would be the best way to deal with the decline of the Roman Empire and the barbarian invasions? Why?

2. How much difference did the barbarian invasions and the collapse of the Empire make to ordinary Roman citizens? Which social groups do you think were affected in what ways? On balance, was the transition beneficial to some?

3. Do you think it is accurate to consider the Early Middle Ages a "dark age"? If our civilization fell, what would a corresponding "dark age" be like?

TRANSITIONS

In "The Empire and Christianity," the course and transformation of the Roman Empire were analyzed. By the fifth century, the Empire in the West fell and Christianity was established as the dominant religion in the Mediterranean area.

In "The Making of Western Europe," the beginnings of a new Western civilization are traced. It, like other new civilizations to the east and south that fell heir to the Classical tradition, differed most fundamentally from its Roman predecessor by being predominantly peasant and dominated by beliefs in an afterlife and hope of personal salvation. Western European peoples combined Germanic and Classical inheritances to form distinctive cultures during the Early Middle Ages, creating a relatively poor, rural, and unstable civilization. This new, Western civilization was supported by the produce of settled peasant family farms, increasingly dominated by a military aristocracy, and committed to the Roman Catholic faith.

In "The Empires of the Early Middle Ages" the rise of Islam, the consolidation of Frankish rule over Western Europe, and the expansion of Christianity in central and Eastern Europe will be examined, as will the reasons why the sizable empires created during this period were unable to cope with new invaders from the East and North.

ANSWERS

Self Test

1c; 2c; 3a; 4d; 5c; 6d; 7a; 8b; 9a; 10d; 11d; 12a; 13b; 14c; 15c; 16b; 17b; 18c

Guide to Documents

I-1b; II-1a; III-1d

Significant Individuals

1g; 2j; 3a; 4l; 5c; 6k; 7e; 8n; 9b; 10m; 11f; 12i; 13h; 14d

Identification

1i; 2p; 3k; 4f; 5n; 6m; 7r; 8d; 9q; 10a; 11e; 12b; 13o; 14g; 15h; 16l; 17c; 18j

SEVEN

THE EMPIRES OF THE EARLY MIDDLE AGES

CHAPTER HIGHLIGHTS

1.   The Byzantine Empire survived by becoming a Greek-speaking bastion of Orthodox Christianity defended by free peasant-soldiers, enriched by trade and manufacturing, and governed by an elaborate bureaucracy.

2.   In the seventh and eighth centuries Islam expanded rapidly, conquering and converting vast areas and developing an advanced urban civilization.

3.   Charlemagne created a Frankish empire that encompassed present-day France, western Germany, and northern Italy that fostered a brief but significant revival of cultural life.

4.   The first East Slavic civilization was organized around the Principality of Kiev, a sophisticated but relatively short-lived state.

5.   From the late ninth to the eleventh century, new incursions by Asiatic nomads in the east and Scandinavian raiders from the north challenged these expansive but unstable states, causing them to crumble into smaller political units more capable of managing local defense.

CHAPTER OUTLINE

I. The Byzantine Empire

1.   Strains on the Empire

2.   Byzantine Government

3.   The Two Churches

4.   Byzantine Economy and Society

5.   Byzantine Culture

6.   Decline of the Byzantine Empire

II. Islam

1.   The Arabs

2.   Muhammad

3.   The Religion of Islam

4.   Expansion of Islam

5.   Islamic Economy and Society

6.   Islamic Culture

7.   Decline of Medieval Islamic Civilization

III. The Carolingian, or Frankish, Empire

1. Charlemagne

2. Carolingian Government

3. The Carolingian Renaissance

4. Carolingian Society and Culture

5. Decline of the Carolingian Empire

IV. The Vikings, Kiev, and England

1. The Vikings

2. The Kievan Rus Principality

3. Anglo-Saxon England

SELF TEST

1. The Emperor Heraclius accomplished all of the following EXCEPT

   a. defeating the Persian Empire.

   b. extending the system of *themes*.

   c. resisting Moslem encroachments.

   d. recapturing the Holy Cross.

2. The *theme* system involved all of the following EXCEPT

   a. giving soldiers and sailor land in exchange for military service.

   b. putting a general, or *strategoi*, in charge of civil administration.

   c. compensating the *strategoi* with a salary and booty rather than land.

   d. expanding the use of slaves, conscripts, and mercenaries.

3. The *theme* system was successful because

   a. soldiers and sailors fought to defend their land, while the *strategoi* remained under Imperial control.

   b. soldiers and sailors fought to gain booty, while the *strategoi* remained under Imperial control.

   c. soldiers and sailors fought to defend their land, while *strategoi* fought to increase their family holdings.

   d. soldiers and sailors fought to gain booty, while the *strategoi* fought to increase their family holdings.

4. The Byzantine Empire's government can best be characterized as

   a. inefficient.

   b. bureaucratic.

   c. arbitrary.

   d. democratic.

5. The Eastern Church and the Roman Church differed in all of the following ways EXCEPT

   a. their doctrines on the relationship between God, Christ, and the Holy Spirit.

   b. the language used in the liturgy.

   c. their desire to expand Christendom through missionary activity.

   d. their relationships to civil authority.

6. Byzantine missionaries had their greatest successes in converting the

   a. Moslems.

   b. Turks.

   c. Slavs.

   d. Persians.

7. The single most important commodity produced by the Byzantine Empire was

   a. wine.

   b. spices.

   c. silk.

   d. gold.

8. Byzantine culture produced significant examples of all of the following EXCEPT

   a. historical scholarship.

   b. religious mosaics.

   c. biblical commentaries.

   d. scientific advances.

9. The social transformations that weakened the Byzantine Empire included all of the following EXCEPT

   a. the increasing power of local landlords.

   b. the decline of the peasantry into serfdom.

   c. the declining authority of the central government.

   d. the growing power of the Church over lay society.

10. The Arabs' were receptive to Muhammad's message because they

   a. were hearty desert nomads, well adapted to their harsh environment.

   b. lived between the stronger powers of Byzantium, Persia, and Abyssinia.

   c. were already in a state of political and religious ferment.

   d. were extremely spirited, tenacious, and formidable warriors.

11. Ideas from which of the following religions are NOT found to any significant extent in Islam?

   a. Christianity.

   b. Judaism.

   c. Hinduism.

   d. Traditional Arab paganism.

12. Muhammad's leadership of Medina affected the nature of his teachings by

    a.   making him intolerant of Christians and Jews.

    b.   focusing him on problems of law and government.

    c.   convincing him that religion and secular affairs cannot be mixed.

    d.   introducing him to Christian, Jewish, and Zoroastrian beliefs.

13. The central tenet of Islam is

    a.   the divine nature of Muhammad.

    b.   the special destiny of the Arabs.

    c.   submission to the will of God.

    d.   the separate role of the clergy.

14. Islam was able to expand rapidly for all of the following reasons EXCEPT

    a.   the Arabs' mastery of desert warfare.

    b.   the religion's easily comprehended beliefs.

    c.   the divisions within Persia and Byzantium.

    d.   Muhammad's inspired military leadership.

15. The Arab conquests had the effect of

    a.   disrupting the civilizations they affected, leading to their gradual but permanent decline.

    b.   creating a new community bound by faith and language and distinguished by economic and cultural vigor.

    c.   creating a series of autonomous cultural areas bound by faith but united by little else.

    d.   transforming the civilizations they affected from cosmopolitan urban to insular rural societies.

16. Medieval Islamic culture made significant advances in all of the following areas EXCEPT

    a.   archeology.

    b.   medicine.

    c.   mathematics.

    d.   philosophy.

17. The resurgence of the West visa vie the Islamic world was signified by all of the following EXCEPT

    a.   the beginning of the reconquest of Spain.

    b.   Christian successes in the Western Mediterranean.

    c.   the Seljuk capture of Baghdad.

    d.   the success of the First Crusade.

18. Charlemagne's success ultimately depended on

    a.   victory in war.

    b.   Papal support.

    c.   his physical presence.

    d.   his deep learning.

19. Charlemagne made his government effective by all of the following EXCEPT

    a. capitalizing on his prestige as Emperor.

    b. traveling widely himself.

    c. sending inspectors to scrutinize a county each year.

    d. creating an elaborate bureaucracy.

20. The Carolingian Renaissance accomplished all of the following EXCEPT

    a. creating an improved handwriting for manuscripts.

    b. establishing a new standard form of Latin.

    c. standardizing religious texts.

    d. creating of an impressive array of monumental buildings.

21. The Carolingian Empire began to decline when it ceased to expand because

    a. the Byzantine Empire seized the opportunity to reassert itself at its expense.

    b. the Popes ceased to back it since it was no longer winning new converts to Christianity.

    c. its constant wars had overtaxed its resources, crippling its economy.

    d. it lost the ability to buy the aristocracy's loyalty with grants of new land.

22. The reasons for the Vikings' widespread expansion include all of the following EXCEPT

    a. The population had grown larger than the available farmland could support.

    b. Chiefs often preferred to emigrate rather than submit when defeated by rivals in war.

    c. Their shallow-draft ships were seaworthy enough for the high seas while able to travel along rivers.

    d. Their strong kings carefully coordinated their attacks to the West, South, and East.

23. The major targets of Viking activity included all of the following EXCEPT

    a. Germany.

    b. France.

    c. Russia.

    d. Britain.

24. Kiev Rus was characterized by all of the following EXCEPT

    a. Fertile agriculture.

    b. Lucrative trade.

    c. Thriving cities.

    d. Fervent Catholicism.

GUIDE TO DOCUMENTS

I. The Koran on Christians and Jews

1. The passage makes all of the following points EXCEPT

    a. Christians, Jews, and others who believe in God and the Last Judgment and act right will be rewarded.

    b. The Koran is the last in a series of Divine revelations that included Moses and Jesus.

    c. Unbelievers will suffer an ignominious punishment.

    d. Pagans have been chosen by Allah for his mercy since his grace is infinite.

2. How might this excerpt help explain the appeal of Islam in the former Byzantine provinces and Spain?

3. How might this view of possible connections between Islam and Christians differ from views held by Christians about possible connections between Christians and Islam?

II. Einhard on Charlemagne

1. The overall impression of Charlemagne that this passage conveys is that he

    a. was more of an intellectual than a man of action.

    b. possessed a formidable original intellect.

    c. combined physical prowess and intellectual curiosity.

    d. had only a superficial interest in intellectual matters.

2. How might one evaluate the objectivity of this description of Charlemagne? Does the author, Einhard, reveal any biases?

SIGNIFICANT INDIVIDUALS

1. Heraclius (HER-a-klē-us)
2. Leo III
3. Charlemagne (SHAR-luh-mān)
4. Oleg
5. Vladimir
6. Yaroslav the Wise
7. Alfred the Great
8. Muhammad
9. Ali (ah-LI)
10. Al-Mamun (al MA-moon)
11. Averroes (ah-VER-ō-ēz)
12. Alcuin (AL-kwin)

a. Kievan ruler who converted to Christianity (r.980-1015)
b. King of Wessex who defeated the Danes (r.871-899)
c. Founder of Islam
d. English scholar who served Charlemagne (735-804)
e. Caliph and patron of philosophy (r.813-833)
f. Frankish king crowned Emperor by the Pope (r.768-814)
g. Unified Novgorad and Kiev into Kiev Rus (r.873?-913)
h. Fourth caliph, central to *Shiite* sect
i. Byzantine Emperor who defeated Persia (r.610-641)
j. Ruler of Kiev at its height (r.1015-1054)
k. Influential Spanish Islamic philosopher (1126?-1198)
l. Byzantine Emperor who started iconoclasm (r.717-741)

IDENTIFICATION

1. iconoclasm
2. "caesaropapism"
   (SĒ-zar-o-pāp-izm)
3. Seljuk Turks (sel-JOOK)
4. Koran (kō-RAN)
5. *hijra* (HIJ-ruh)
6. Mecca (MEK-a)
7. Umayyad (oo-MĪ-ad)
8. *Sunnites* (SOON-īts)
9. *Shiites* (SHĒ-īts)
10. zero
11. county
12. *missi dominici*
13. *Danelaw* (DĀN-law)
14. Carolingian minuscule
    (kar-ō-LIN-jē-an mi-NUS-kyool)

a. Basic administrative area of Carolingian Empire
b. Governmental system in which an emperor rules both church and state
c. Islamic dissident party of Ali
d. Charlemagne's traveling inspectors
e. Handwriting using both upper and lower case letters
f. Mathematical concept developed by Islamic scholars
g. Muhammad's trip from Mecca to Medina
h. Book with the word of God as reported by Muhammad
i. Home of Muhammad and holiest city of Islam
j. Byzantine movement to destroy religious images
k. The part of England ruled by Vikings
l. First dynasty that ruled Islamic world
m. Islamic group that follows tradition as well as Koran
n. Asiatic peoples who crippled the Byzantine empire and vanquished the Abbasid caliphate

CHRONOLOGICAL DIAGRAM

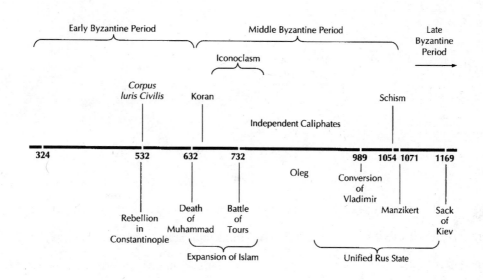

MAP EXERCISES

1.   Label, around the year 800, the Frankish Empire under Charlemagne, the Byzantine Empire, and Islam.

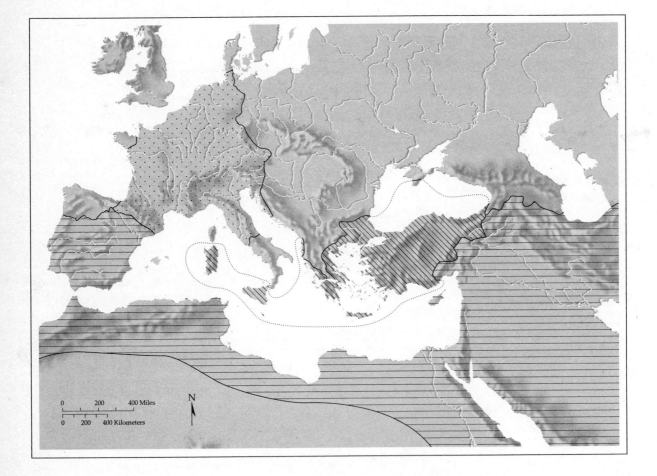

1. Indicate the homelands of the invading Vikings, Saracens, and Magyars; and show which arrows of invasions delineate routes taken by each of these three groups between the eighth and tenth centuries.

2. What does this map reveal about the political strength and vulnerability of Western Europe during these centuries?

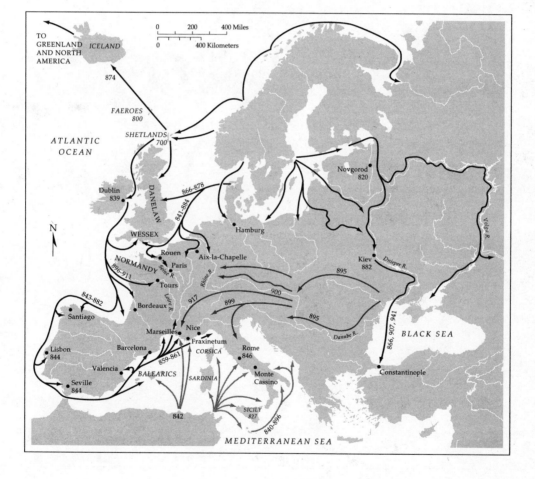

1. Outline the boundaries of the Principality of Kiev in the eleventh century. Indicate the locations of Novgorod, Moscow, and the city of Kiev.

PROBLEMS FOR ANALYSIS

I. The Byzantine Empire

1. Why was the Byzantine Empire able to survive and expand during the Early Middle Ages?

2. Compare the Eastern and the Western Churches. How did their connections to secular authority differ?

3. Explain the decline of the Byzantine Empire.

II. Islam

1. How do you explain the extremely rapid spread of Islam in the seventh century? Was it mainly due to the nature of the religion? What role did the characteristics and environment of the Arabs play in this? Was it simply a function of conquest?

2. Compare the cosmopolitan Islamic civilization with the civilization of Western Europe during the Early Middle Ages. How did they differ politically and culturally?

3. In some ways Islam significantly influenced the West, yet some historians argue that the two civilizations were fundamentally separate. Do you agree? Why?

III. The Carolingian or Frankish Empire

1. How were Carolingian leaders able to acquire power from their Merovingian predecessors and establish an extensive kingdom? Why was this kingdom short-lived?

2. What were the principal characteristics of the Carolingian Renaissance? Which of these were most important and why?

IV. The Vikings, Kiev, and England

1. How were the Vikings' activities in Western Europe similar to, and how were they different from, their activities in Eastern Europe? How do you explain the differences?

2. Should the Principality of Kiev be considered one of the most advanced civilizations of its time? Why?

SPECULATIONS

1. Suppose the Western Roman Empire survived in a shrunken form—confined to Italy and areas bordering the Mediterranean in France, Spain, and northwestern Africa. Speculate on how this might have changed the course of European and Islamic history.

TRANSITIONS

In "The Making of Western Europe," the development of a new civilization in the West from a mixture of "barbarian" and Roman peoples during the first half of the Early Middle Ages was examined.

"The Empires of the Early Middle Ages" shifts the focus to the extensive empires that rose and declined during the second half of the period. The Byzantine Empire preserved the Eastern portion of the old Roman Empire by transforming it. However, it lost significant territories to the Muslims, who exploded across southwest Asia and north Africa all the way to Spain, bringing these vast territories a new religion and ushering them into a Golden Age. Charlemagne's Frankish Empire temporarily restored unity to Western Europe, while Kiev Rus established a settled state in western Russia for the first time. Each of these empires, however, suffered from internal weaknesses and external challenges, and by the end of the period all were either gone or in significant decline.

In "Restoration of an Ordered Society," we will examine the social, economic, political, and religious changes that led to a more firmly established civilization in Western Europe after the year 1000.

ANSWERS

Self Test

1c; 2d; 3a; 4b; 5c; 6c; 7c; 8d; 9d; 10c; 11c; 12b; 13c; 14d; 15b; 16a; 17c; 18a; 19d; 20d; 21d; 22d; 23a; 24d

Guide to Documents

I-1d; II-1c

Significant Individuals

1i; 2l; 3f; 4g; 5a; 6j; 7b; 8c; 9h; 10e; 11k; 12d

Identification

1j; 2b; 3n; 4h; 5g; 6i; 7l; 8m; 9c; 10f; 11a; 12d; 13k; 14e

EIGHT
RESTORATION OF AN ORDERED SOCIETY

CHAPTER HIGHLIGHTS

1. By the 1000s, Western Europe's agriculture was flourishing, its population was expanding, commerce was increasing, and towns and cities were beginning to grow.

2. European society stabilized through the spread of feudal institutions and the rule of more effective kings.

3. The clergy and papacy gained in strength and influence through reform of the Church.

4. The crusades, initiated for a variety of reasons, led to an expansion of Europeans into the East.

CHAPTER OUTLINE

I. Economic and Social Changes

1. Manorialism

2. Peasant Life

3. Feudalism

4. Life of the Nobility

5. Expansion of Europe

6. Commercial Expansion

7. Rebirth of Urban Life

II. Governments of Europe 1000-1150

1. England

2. Capetian France

3. The German Empire

III. The Reform of the Western Church

1. The Church in Crisis

2. Monastic Reform

3. Papal Reform

4. Investiture Controversy

5. Consolidation of Papal Reform

IV. The Crusades

1. Origins

2. The Motives of the Crusaders

3. The First Crusade

4. The Kingdom of Jerusalem

5. The Later Crusades

6. Military-Religious Orders

7. Results of the Crusades

SELF TEST

1. A manor was all of the following EXCEPT

   a. a community of peasants.

   b. a jurisdiction under the authority of a lord.

   c. a unit of church government.

   d. an economic unit.

2. Gender roles among peasants

   a. were relatively undifferentiated.

   b. made women the primary farm workers.

   c. divided the work between the sexes.

   d. left women free to care for their children.

3. Feudalism involved all of the following EXCEPT

   a. a commitment by a vassal to serve his lord in war and by giving council.

   b. a commitment by a lord to defend his vassal militarily and in legal proceedings.

   c. the grant by a lord of a fief, control of land and its peasants, to his vassal.

   d. a payment by the vassal to the lord as rent for his fief.

4. Primogeniture (bequeathing a family's entire estate to the eldest son) had a strong impact on Europe because

   a. it caused a wave of assassinations as younger siblings sought to secure the family fortune for themselves.

   b. it forced younger sons to seek their fortunes as freebooters, as Church officials, or as crusaders.

   c. it made it impossible for girls to get dowries to insure a suitable marriage.

   d. it turned the younger generation against the older.

5. Europeans coped with the growth of population in all of the following ways EXCEPT

   a. clearing forests and draining swamps.

   b. settling in the lands won by the Crusades.

   c. emigrating to eastern Europe.

   d. settling lands reconquered in Spain.

6. Which of the following was NOT a major trading zone in Medieval Europe?

   a. The Mediterranean zone connecting southern Europe with North Africa and the Middle East.

   b. The Northern zone encompassing the Baltic and North Seas.

   c. The Atlantic zone that connected Northern Europe with North Africa and the Middle East.

   d. The Overland zone that joined the Mediterranean and Northern zones.

7. The principal urban classes in the eleventh and early twelfth centuries included all of the following EXCEPT

   a. wealthy patricians.

   b. local merchants.

   c. shopkeepers.

   d. artisanal workers.

8. The most important event of the period for England's government was

   a. the Norman conquest.

   b. the final defeat of the Vikings.

   c. the creation of the *Domesday Book*.

   d. Henry I's administrative reforms.

9. The Capetian dynasty was able to establish itself by

   a. aggressive conquests.

   b. clever marriages.

   c. fortunate childbearing.

   d. widespread bribery.

10. The German ruler was the preeminent monarch for of all of the following reasons EXCEPT

    a. the extent of the territories he ruled.

    b. his status as "Roman Emperor."

    c. his power in Italy as well as Germany.

    d. his dynasty's secure claim to the throne.

11. All of the following were problems of the Church needing reform EXCEPT

    a. the excessive authority of the Pope.

    b. the sale of Church offices and services.

    c. lay dominion over Church offices and lands.

    d. the failure of the clergy to remain celibate.

12. The Cluniac movement helped reform monasteries because it

    a. placed monasteries under the Pope and the Abbot of Cluny rather than local lords.

    b. broke the hold of the Papacy on appointments to monastic leadership.

    c. forced the Emperor to appeal to the Pope for support against his enemies in Germany.

    d. it closed corrupt monasteries and distributed their members among reformed houses.

13. The reforming popes of the eleventh century accomplished all of the following EXCEPT

    a.   strengthening Papal supervision of the Church.

    b.   freeing the papacy from military dependence on the Emperor.

    c.   transferring much control over Church appointments from lay officials to Churchmen.

    d.   ending warfare among Christians by sponsoring the Crusades.

14. The investiture controversy was a struggle

    a.   to control the Church's lucrative investments.

    b.   to control Church appointments.

    c.   to invest the College of Cardinals with the authority to elect popes.

    d.   over the Emperors' cynical attempts to appoint corrupt popes.

15. Twelfth century popes consolidated Papal reforms by all of the following EXCEPT

    a.   strengthening the voice of Church councils.

    b.   sponsoring the codification of canon law.

    c.   expanding the Church's central bureaucracy.

    d.   extending the Church's judicial authority.

16. The origins of the crusades included all of the following EXCEPT

    a.   the taxes and tolls the Seljuk Turks charged Christian pilgrims to the Holy Lands.

    b.   the moves by the Seljuk Turks to prevent Christian pilgrims from reaching Palestine.

    c.   the disastrous defeat of the Byzantine Empire by the Seljuk Turks at Manzikert.

    d.   the desire of the Byzantine Emperor for Norman mercenaries in his counter-offensive.

17. The motives of the Crusaders included all of the following EXCEPT a desire to

    a.   win land and serfs.

    b.   do God's work.

    c.   gain farmland for their peasants.

    d.   gain God's favor.

18. The First Crusade can be termed

    a.   a costly stalemate.

    b.   a humiliating failure.

    c.   a resounding success.

    d.   a calculated compromise.

19. The crusader states survived in Palestine for about

    a.   2 years.

    b.   20 years.

    c.   200 years.

    d.   2000 years.

20. The Fourth Crusade accomplished all of the following EXCEPT

   a. conquering the Christian city of Zara for Venice.

   b. capturing and sacking Constantinople.

   c. crippling the Byzantine Empire.

   d. reaching the Holy Lands.

21. The military-religious orders established during the crusades included all of the following EXCEPT

   a. the Templars.

   b. The Hospitalers.

   c. The Knights of Jerusalem.

   d. The Teutonic Knights.

22. The crusades stimulated Europe in all of the following ways EXCEPT

   a. castle design and siege techniques.

   b. expanded trade and manufacturing.

   c. increased reliance on indirect taxes.

   d. heightened awareness of exotic cultures.

GUIDE TO DOCUMENTS

I. A Twelfth-Century Description of London

1. This passage implies that in the twelfth century public eateries were still

   a. uncommon.

   b. filthy.

   c. expensive.

   d. slow.

2. What made London a particularly suitable location for the "cook shop" described in the passage?

II. Louis VI Subdues a Violent Baron

1. According to the passage, all of the following weapons helped the Church protect its interests EXCEPT

   a. excommunication.

   b. royal support.

   c. great wealth.

   d. divine aid.

2. What sorts of challenges to authority were presented to monarchs, and in what ways might monarchs meet those challenges, as revealed by this document?

III. Gregory VII's Letter to the German Nobility after Canossa

1. Gregory states that he removed the excommunication from Henry because

    a. he was moved by Henry's tears.

    b. others accused him of being too harsh.

    c. he had tired of admonishing Henry.

    d. Henry implemented the policies he desired.

2. What does this passage show about the relationship of the Pope to the Emperor?

SIGNIFICANT INDIVIDUALS

1. Harold Godwin	a.	Founder of the French dynasty that became hereditary
2. William the Conqueror	b.	Crusader King of Jerusalem (r.1100-1118)
3. Henry I	c.	Muslim leader who recaptured Jerusalem (r.1189-1192)
4. Hugh Capet (ka-PE)	d.	Strong Emperor who reformed Church (r.1039-1056)
5. Louis VI	e.	English king who reformed administration (r.1100-1135)
6. Otto I	f.	Norman adventurer in southern Italy (d.1085)
7. Henry III	g.	Abbess, poet, playwright, and historian (ca.937-1004)
8. Henry IV	h.	Last Anglo-Saxon king of England (r.1066)
9. Robert Guiscard (GWĒZ-kard)	i.	French scholar who became Pope Sylvester II (d.1003)
10. Baldwin	j.	Pope who humbled the Emperor (r.1073-1085)
11. Saladin (SAL-ah-din)	k.	Saxon king who became Emperor (r. 936-973)
12. Gregory VII	l.	Norman duke who won English throne (r.1066-1087)
13. Gerbert of Aurillac (OR-il-lac)	m.	Emperor who struggled against Pope (r.1056-1106)
14. Roswitha of Gandersheim	n.	French king who subdued petty nobles (r.1108-1137)

IDENTIFICATION

1. manor
2. demesne (di-MĀN)
3. serf
4. vassal
5. fief (fēf)
6. subinfeudation
7. castellan (KAS-te-lan)
8. internal colonization
9. *Drang nach Osten*
   (drahng nakh-AH-stin)
10. *Reconquista* (reh-kon-KIS-ta)
11. "spices"
12. Champagne (sham-PĀN)
13. justices in eyre (air)
14. simony
15. Cluny (KLU-nē)
16. investiture controversy
17. canon law

a. German "drive to the east"
b. The process by which a fief was subdivided
c. Itinerant judges used by English kings to expand power
d. The practice of selling Church offices and services
e. Subordinate of a lord
f. A Medieval agricultural estate ruled by a lord
g. Monastery at heart of tenth century reform movement
h. Dispute between Emperor and Pope
i. Province where trade fairs were held year-round

j. The lord's portion of farmland, worked by peasants
k. Statements of Bible, Church councils, fathers, and popes
l. Owner of a castle
m. The process of clearing forests and draining swamps
n. Land granted by a lord to a vassal
o. Peasant bound to the estate where he lived
p. Christian reconquest of Iberia
q. Goods from the East

CHRONOLOGICAL DIAGRAM

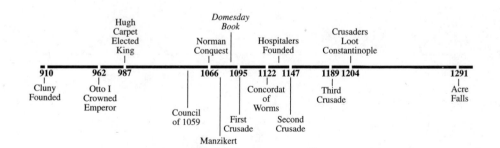

MAP EXERCISE

1.   Label the main trading zones of Europe, and trace the major routes connecting them.
2.   Indicate the location of the Crusader kingdoms.

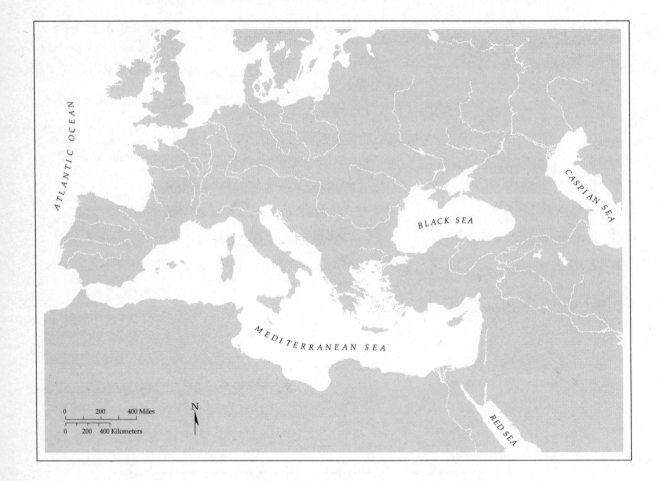

PROBLEMS FOR ANALYSIS

I. Economic and Social Changes

1. What were the distinguishing features of manorialism? In what ways did the system meet the needs of the peasants and the needs of the lords? Who benefited most from it?

2. Why was feudalism effective in promoting social order in Europe during the eleventh and twelfth centuries? What was the cement that held feudal relations together?

3. Explain the causes and significance of the population changes that occurred during the eleventh and twelfth centuries.

4. In what ways was there a revival of commerce and urban life during this period? Who benefited from this?

II. Governments of Europe

1. Compare the development of government in England, France, and Germany. In what ways was it the same? How was it different? How do you account for the similarities and differences?

III. The Reform of the Western Church

1. What conditions created a need for reform within the Western Church?

2. What roles did popes and Cluniac monasticism play in the reform of the Church? What was so "reforming" about their activities?

IV. The Crusades

1. What circumstances led to the First Crusades? What balance of religious, economic, and social motives do you think led people to participate in these crusades?

2. Considering the effort involved and the result of the crusades, were they a success or a failure? Why?

3. What were the most important consequences of the crusades? Is it fair to argue that the crusades proved to be of greater economic than religious significance for Europe? Why?

SPECULATIONS

1. Do you think there is something special about the year 1000? Explain.

2. What policies would you recommend to an eleventh-century king to maximize his power? Why?

3. Should we consider the Church special, or is it just an institution with problems like the government or any other institution? Support your view historically?

4. Considering your knowledge of the crusades, what sort of cause might lead you to join a "crusade"? What would your motives be?

TRANSITIONS

"The Empires of the Early Middle Ages" traced the rise and decline of the expansive states that appeared in the centuries before 100.

In "Restoration of an Ordered Society" focus is on the vigorous period of growth in the eleventh and early twelfth centuries. Economic arrangements, government, and religious institutions all achieved a stability and vitality that launched Western Europe on a sustained process of development and enabled it to expand to the South and East.

In "The Flowering of Medieval Civilization" the civilization of the Middle Ages is at its peak and faces new problems.

ANSWERS

Self Test

1c; 2c; 3d; 4b; 5b; 6c; 7d; 8a; 9c; 10d; 11a; 12a; 13d; 14b; 15a; 16b; 17c; 18c; 19c; 20d; 21c; 22c

Guide to Documents

I-1a; II-1c; III-1b

Significant Individuals

1h; 2l; 3e; 4a; 5n; 6k; 7d; 8m; 9f; 10b; 11c; 12j; 13i; 14g

Identification

1f; 2j; 3o; 4e; 5n; 6b; 7l; 8m; 9a; 10p; 11q; 12i; 13c; 14d; 15g; 16h; 17k

NINE
THE FLOWERING OF MEDIEVAL CIVILIZATION

CHAPTER HIGHLIGHTS

1. The late twelfth and early thirteenth centuries saw a tremendous invigoration of European culture with the rise of universities, the development of scholastic theology, the evolution of Romanesque architecture into the soaring Gothic style, and the creation of an elaborate court culture.

2. The kings of England, France, and Iberia used their legal prerogatives to enhance their power by formalizing feudal principals into governmental ones. The German emperors, in contrast, traded their legal prerogatives in Germany for support of their futile campaigns in Italy.

3. The English barons forced King John to recognize his own subordination to the law in the Magna Carta, the foundation of English, and American, civil rights.

4. The Church faced its first major heretical challenges since antiquity, and responded with organizational innovation, repression, and a reaffirmation of its fundamental tenets.

CHAPTER OUTLINE

I. Cultural Developments

1. The Rise of Universities

2. Scholasticism

3. Spiritual Approaches to Knowledge

4. Romanesque Architecture

5. The Gothic Style

6. Court Culture

II. The States of Europe

1. England

2. France

3. The Iberian Kingdoms

4. The Holy Roman Empire

III. The Church

1. The Growth of Heresy

2. The Suppression of Heresy

3. The Franciscans

4. Papal Government

SELF TEST

1. The founding of universities was important for all of the following reasons EXCEPT

   a. they supplied Church and state with literate officials.

   b. they nurtured the rise of rationalism in the Scholastic movement.

   c. they created an institutional setting for teaching and research that has spread throughout the world.

   d. they gave students a chance to party hearty before entering the real world.

2. Abelard's *Sic et Non* achieved its effect by all of the following EXCEPT

   a. showing that statements from the Bible, Church councils, and Church fathers contradicted each other.

   b. leaving the contradictory statements of Church authorities unresolved in embarrassing juxtaposition.

   c. implying that dialectic analysis was necessary to reconcile the statements of Church authorities.

   d. demonstrating that his love of Heloise that had led him to understand the true nature of Christianity.

3. The recovery of Aristotle's full body of works was important to Medieval intellectual life because it

   a. gave Christians renewed respect for the Muslims who translated and commented on it.

   b. challenged Christians to reconcile his rational and naturalistic philosophy with Christian revelation.

   c. demonstrated that reason could be used to deduce the articles of faith of the Christian religion.

   d. proved that reason could be used to deduce the characteristics of the natural world.

4. Thomas Aquinas's *Summa Theologica* attempted to provide all of the following EXCEPT

   a. a comprehensive introduction to Christian theology.

   b. a systematic view of the universe.

   c. a model of the way that direct observation leads to truth.

   d. a reconciliation of natural, revealed, pagan and Christian truth.

5. Women played their most prominent role in Medieval religion as

   a. surrogates for Mary.

   b. anchorites and mystics.

   c. students and professors.

   d. priestesses.

6. Romanesque cathedrals were distinguished by all of the following EXCEPT

   a. rounded arches.

   b. fantastic sculptures.

   c. stone roofs.

   d. large stained glass windows.

7. Gothic cathedrals were distinguished by all of the following EXCEPT

    a.   pointed arches.

    b.   fantastic sculptures.

    c.   flying buttresses.

    d.   large stained glass windows.

8. The court culture that developed in the twelfth century involved all of the following EXCEPT

    a.   a refined code of conduct for knights.

    b.   a preoccupation with romantic love.

    c.   a respect for people from all classes.

    d.   a literature celebrating love and heroism.

9. English "common law" is based on

    a.   the laws common to all nations.

    b.   Roman law.

    c.   the will of the commoners.

    d.   the precedent set by earlier cases.

10. The Magna Carta was most important because it

    a.   stated the principals upon which modern liberty is based.

    b.   established legal limits on the power of the king.

    c.   resolved the technical problems of feudal law.

    d.   addressed the concerns of the entire English population.

11. During this period, the French monarchy accomplished all of the following EXCEPT

    a.   making itself unquestioned master of the Ile-de-France.

    b.   greatly enlarging the royal demesne.

    c.   extending royal justice into the feudal principalities.

    d.   securing the right to levy taxes throughout the country.

12. Which of the following was NOT a major Christian kingdom in Iberia?

    a.   Aragon.

    b.   Castile.

    c.   Grenada.

    d.   Portugal.

13. The Emperor who conferred sovereignty to local German governments in order to pursue his goals in Italy was

    a.   Frederick I Barbarossa.

    b.   Henry VI.

    c.   Frederick II Hohenstaufen.

    d.   Manfred.

14. All of the following contributed to the growth of heresy EXCEPT

    a. the corruption of the Church.

    b. the Pope's refusal to call a new Church council.

    c. the desire of lay people to participate in religion.

    d. the discontents of the poor and of women.

15. The Waldensians and the Albigensians shared all of the following EXCEPT

    a. rejection of material things.

    b. denial of the validity of the sacraments.

    c. denunciation of the corruption of the clergy.

    d. belief that two cosmic principals compete for supremacy.

16. The Church responded to heresy by all of the following EXCEPT

    a. founding the Dominican and the Franciscan orders to preach among the people.

    b. setting up the Inquisition and launching a crusade.

    c. clarifying and reaffirming the basic tenets of the Catholic faith.

    d. recasting the role of the clergy in response to the heretic's complaints.

17. The Franciscans differed from the Waldensians in that

    a. its members embraced poverty.

    b. its members preached to the laity.

    c. it accepted the validity of the sacraments.

    d. it was started by a charismatic preacher.

18. All of the following were true of the Inquisition EXCEPT

    a. it accepted secret denunciations and kept accusers' names secret.

    b. suspects had no right to counsel and could be tortured.

    c. it included incompetent and even demented judges.

    d. it executed hundreds of convicted heretics.

19. Innocent III pursued all of the following goals EXCEPT

    a. the eradication of heresy.

    b. the hegemony of the papacy.

    c. the repression of Scholasticism.

    d. the clarification of doctrine.

GUIDE TO DOCUMENTS

I. Abelard's "Sic et Non"

1. According to the passage, undeniable truth is conveyed by all of the following EXCEPT

    a.   certain reason.

    b.   canonical authority.

    c.   the scriptures.

    d.   the holy spirit.

2. In what ways might Abelard's Scholasticism be seen as encouraging analytical thought in general?

II. Excerpts from "Magna Carta"

1. This document places all of the following restraints on the king of England EXCEPT

    a.   he cannot impose taxes without the consent of the realm.

    b.   he cannot infringe upon the traditional liberties of the cities and towns.

    c.   he cannot embark on a foreign war without the consent of the realm.

    d.   he cannot prosecute anyone without just cause and legal basis.

2. Which of these provisions might, in the long run, become the basis for common law rights for everyone?

III. The Techniques of the Inquisition

1. According to this document, the beliefs of the Church that heretics might disagree with included all EXCEPT

    a.   the trinity of the one God: Father, Son, and Holy Spirit.

    b.   that Christ was born, died, and was resurrected.

    c.   that bread and wine change into the body and blood of Christ during mass.

    d.   that oaths are unlawful and the sin is born by whomever originates them.

2. In what ways did the Church, through inquisitors such as Bernard Gui, attempt to combat heresy?

SIGNIFICANT INDIVIDUALS

1. St. Anselm
2. Peter Abelard (AB-e-lard)
3. Thomas Aquinas (a-KWĬ-nuhs)
4. John Duns Scotus (SKŎ-tes)
5. Marie de France
6. Henry II
7. Eleanor of Aquitaine (AK-wi-tān)
8. Richard I, the Lion-Hearted
9. John I
10. Philip II Augustus
11. St. Louis IX
12. Frederick I Barbarossa (bar-be-ROS-a)
13. Frederick II Hohenstaufen (HŎ-en-shtou-fen)
14. Peter Waldo
15. Innocent III
16. St. Francis of Assisi (a-SĔ-zĕ)

a. Author of short romance narratives (d.1210)
b. English king who ruled much of France (r.1154-1189)
c. French king noted for his piety (r.1226-1270)
d. First thinker to apply dialectic to theology (1033-1109)
e. Leader of the Waldensian heresy (12th century)
f. Emperor who gave up Germany for Italy (r.1212-1250)
g. Theologian who argued logical priority of faith to reason (1265?-1308)
h. French king who regained Normandy (r.1180-1223)
i. Brilliant theologian and unfortunate lover (1079-1142)
j. Emperor who worked to control Germany(r.1152-1190)
k. Pope who organized the struggle against heresy.
l. English king who preferred fighting to ruling (r.1189-1199)
m. Queen of France and England and cultural leader (1137-1189)
n. Founder of Franciscan order (1182?-1226)
o. Greatest Scholastic theologian (1225?-1274)
p. English king who granted the Magna Carta (r.1199-1216)

IDENTIFICATION

1.	Scholasticism	a.	Spanish representative assembly
2.	*Summa Theologica* (SOOM-uh thē-uh LOJ-i-kuh)	b.	Heretic who believed in the struggle between a good god and an evil god, with the latter ruler of the material world
3.	Romanesque	c.	Singer specializing in lyric poetry for courtly audience
4.	Gothic	d.	Arm of Church charged with investigating heresy
5.	Chivalry	e.	Itinerant salaried French royal official
6.	Vernacular	f.	Heretical follower of Peter Waldo
7.	Troubadour	g.	Architectural style characterized by pointed arches
8.	Magna Carta	h.	Church body that defined sacraments and made reforms
9.	*Bailli* (bayi)	i.	Body of writing based on dialectic applied to Christianity
10.	*Cortes* (KŎR-tez)	j.	Thomas Aquinas' scholastic masterpiece
11.	Waldensian	k.	The constitutional foundation of English liberties
12.	Albigensian (al-beh-JEN-sē-en)	l.	Refined code of conduct for knights
13.	Inquisition	m.	Architectural style characterized by rounded arches
14.	Fourth Lateran Council	n.	Language of everyday speech, as opposed to Latin

CHRONOLOGICAL DIAGRAM

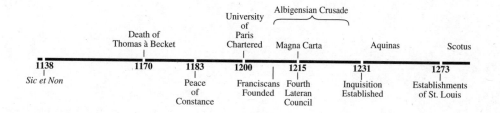

MAP EXERCISE

1.   Label the main political units of Europe toward the end of the twelfth century.

2.   What sorts of problems would France have to overcome before unifying the territory that would become modern France?

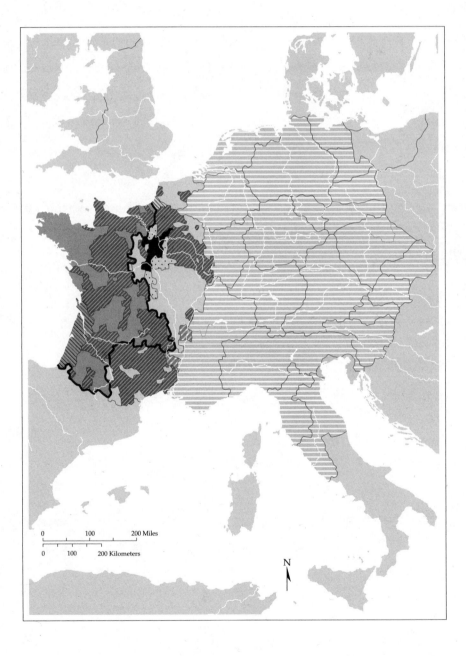

PROBLEMS FOR ANALYSIS

I. Cultural Developments

1. Compare the universities and student life around 1200 with those of today. What was so important about the development of universities at this early date?

2. Compare the ideas of Aquinas and Duns Scotus. How does the analysis of Duns Scotus signify a change from the synthesis of Aquinas?

3. Did religious concerns completely dominate cultural life during the eleventh and twelfth centuries? Support your argument.

II. The States of Europe

1. The Magna Carta is sometimes thought of as a democratic document. In light of the political developments in England during the thirteenth century, do you agree? Why?

2. Compare constitutional consolidation in France with the disintegration of the Holy Roman Empire. How do you explain the differences?

III. The Church

1. Does the growth of heresy, and its suppression, indicate that the Church was effectively unified at the beginning of the thirteenth century? Why?

2. Compare the factors that evidenced the growing strength of the Church with those that evidenced future problems for the Church.

SPECULATIONS

1. If you could select any time between 400 and 1400 to live in, would you select the decades around 1200? What would the advantages and disadvantages be?

2. If you were a pope around 1200, what policies would you follow to promote the best interests of the Church?

TRANSITIONS

In "Restoration of an Ordered Society" the quickening pace of economic, political, and religious life in the West from 1000 to 1150 was traced.

"The Flowering of Medieval Civilization," focuses on the period between 1150 and 1250. During most of this time Europe enjoyed relative prosperity, peace, institutional stability, and intellectual advancement. The period saw tremendous development, and laid the foundations for more to come.

"The Urban Economy and the Consolidation of States," will focus on the ways in which the European economy, society, political systems, and religious life further developed in the years between 1250 and 1348.

ANSWERS

Self Test

1d; 2d; 3b; 4c; 5b; 6d; 7b; 8c; 9d; 10b; 11d; 12c; 13c; 14b; 15d; 16d; 17c; 18d; 19c

Guide to Documents

I-1c; II-1c; III-1d

Significant Individuals

1d; 2i; 3o; 4g; 5a; 6b; 7m; 8l; 9p; 10h; 11c; 12j; 13f; 14e; 15k; 16n

Identification

1i; 2j; 3m; 4g; 5l; 6n; 7c; 8k; 9e; 10a; 11f; 12b; 13d; 14h

TEN
THE URBAN ECONOMY AND THE CONSOLIDATION OF STATES

CHAPTER HIGHLIGHTS

1. Commerce and industry expanded greatly from the twelfth to the thirteenth century, fueling the growth in number, size, independence, and importance of towns.

2. In the various states of Europe, representative assemblies gained power, and constitutional stability improved.

3. In the East, the Byzantine Empire reestablished itself as a significant, although reduced, power, while the Moscow used Mongol overlordship to create the kernel of the modern Russian state.

4. Corruption and involvement in politics decreased the prestige of the Papacy, while lay piety grew stronger.

5. Dante's *Divine Comedy*, perhaps the greatest synthesis of Medieval culture, combined Scholasticism, courtly romance, spiritual journey, classical learning, and contemporary politics.

CHAPTER OUTLINE

I. Cities, Trade, and Commerce

1. Urban Government

2. The Organization of Crafts

3. The Guilds

4. Business Institutions

5. Navigation

6. Urban Life

II. Monarchies and the Development of Representative Institutions

1. England and the Development of Parliament

2. France

3. The Holy Roman Empire

III. Government in the East

1. The Byzantine Empire

2. The Mongols

3. Russia

IV. The Papacy and the Church

1. The Papacy

2. Lay Religious Observance

V. Learning and Literature

1. Philosophy (12.5, 374)

2. Dante (9.4, 278)

SELF TEST

1. Towns gained independence for all of the following reasons EXCEPT

    a. kings wanted them as counterweights to the nobles.

    b. the Church needed towns as seats for bishoprics.

    c. towns won their rights by armed insurrection.

    d. nobles wanted the wealth that free towns produced.

2. Towns regulated the lives of their people in all of the following ways EXCEPT

    a. sanitation.

    b. weapons.

    c. education.

    d. business practices.

3. The biggest industry in most Medieval towns was

    a. brewing beer.

    b. making wool cloth.

    c. banking.

    d. making linen cloth.

4. The putting out system involved

    a. expelling workers who failed to produce quality goods.

    b. regulation of bath houses.

    c. having each step in production performed by a specialist.

    d. enterprises like mines, construction, and the Venice arsenal.

5. Guilds did all of the following EXCEPT

    a. promote the interests of the commercial classes.

    b. foster entrepreneurial initiative by encouraging free competition.

    c. set standards, provided for members' welfare, and performed civic activities.

    d. regulated the apprentice system which educated young people for craft work.

6. All of the following were business innovations of the time EXCEPT

    a. banks.

    b. double-entry bookkeeping

    c. permanent partnerships.

    d. maritime insurance.

7. The main importance of improved navigation to twelfth century Europe was it made possible

    a. voyages of exploration.

    b. naval victories over the Muslims.

    c. more efficient trade.

    d. widespread travel.

8. Urban life was characterized by all of the following EXCEPT

    a. cramped and overcrowded quarters.

    b. few unmarried adults.

    c. dirt and disease.

    d. a steady flow of immigrants.

9. The Medieval English parliament did all of the following EXCEPT

    a. approve new taxes.

    b. act as the highest court.

    c. depose unsuccessful kings.

    d. help collect taxes.

10. The English parliament was important because it

    a. enabled the English monarchy to win its wars against France.

    b. established a mechanism for English subjects to participate in government.

    c. established the separation of judicial, legislative, and executive branches of government.

    d. led to the early end to the monarchy and establishment of a modern republic.

11. The fact that Philip the Fair's ministers were schooled in Roman law was important because it led them to

    a. try to resurrect the representative principals of Roman politics through the Estates General.

    b. insist that the all Frenchmen, including the king, were subject to the laws of France.

    c. believe that his rule would only be effective if he controlled the ruler of Rome, the Pope.

    d. consider him "emperor in his own land," subject to no higher power on earth.

12. Philip the Fair raised money in all of the following ways EXCEPT

    a. confiscating the property of the Jews.

    b. imprisoning foreign merchants to extort money from them.

    c. taking subsidies from Edward I.

    d. persecuting the Knights Templar as heretics in order to confiscate their property.

13. The Golden Bull of 1356 had the effect of

    a. solidifying the Pope's control of the selection of the German Emperor.

    b. confirming the Luxemburg dynasty's control of the German Empire.

    c. institutionalizing the elective, and hence weak, basis of the Emperor's power.

    d. enabling the Habsburg family to dominate the German Empire from then on.

14. The Mongols conquered in all of the following EXCEPT

    a.   China.

    b.   Persia.

    c.   Byzantium.

    d.   Russia.

15. Ivan I increased the power of Muscovy by all of the following EXCEPT

    a.   collecting tribute for the Mongols from the other Russians.

    b.   forcing Novgorod to submit and annexing it and its territories.

    c.   encouraging the primate of Russia to make Moscow his residence.

    d.   extending its territory along the Moscow River and to the north.

16. All of the following problems beset the Papacy in the thirteenth century EXCEPT

    a.   financial pressures induced it to adopt corrupt measures to raise money that then discredited it.

    b.   the Catholic cults of holy relics were attacked by crusaders influenced by Byzantine iconoclasm.

    c.   Clement V and his successors' residence at Avignon reduced its credibility as an independent voice.

    d.   the revocation of Boniface VIII's *Unam Sanctam* signified the waxing strength of secular rulers.

17. The Church attempted to deal with lay piety by

    a.   reforming itself in order to reassert its spiritual leadership.

    b.   suppressing all unsanctioned lay religiosity as heresy.

    c.   opening the Church hierarchy to spiritually inspired laymen.

    d.   tolerating it and trying to channel it into approved institutions.

18. Medieval philosophers contributed to modern science in all of the following ways EXCEPT

    a.   demonstrating that celestial bodies must be made of the same matter as earth.

    b.   suggesting that the movement of the planets could be better explained by assuming the earth is in motion.

    c.   formulating the principal that a simple explanation is superior to a complex one.

    d.   devising the experimental method in which an hypothesis is subjected to empirical tests.

GUIDE TO DOCUMENTS

I. The Craft of Weavers of Silk Kerchiefs at Paris

1. This selection shows that Medieval industry

    a.   produced poor quality.

    b.   was highly regulated.

    c.   involved mainly women.

    d.   exploited the workers.

2. What was the purpose of each of the regulations? What was their overall effect?

II. Unam Sanctam

1. The pope claims all of the following in this document EXCEPT

    a. Church and state are like sword and sheath.

    b. kings are subordinate to priests.

    c. priests are subordinate to the Pope.

    d. the Pope answers only to God.

2. How does the pope justify these claims?

3. What would secular powers give up by accepting these claims?

III. The Beguinage of Saint Elizabeth in Ghent (1328)

1. The passage conveys all of the following information about the Beguines EXCEPT

    a. they lived simply.

    b. they supported themselves.

    c. they only worked together..

    d. some members supervised the others.

2. How did a Beguinage compare to a traditional monastery or nunnery? In what ways was it similar? In what ways different?

IDENTIFICATION

1.	putting-out system	a.	Loan in which repayment was in a higher value currency
2.	guilds	b.	English representative body
3.	apprentice	c.	Division of Mongol empire that ruled Russia
4.	usury	d.	Russian emperor
5.	bill of exchange	e.	Quasi-monastic groups of pious lay women
6.	*compagnia* (kom-PA-nĕ-ya)	f.	Lands between the Volga and the Okra rivers
7.	Alfonsine Tables (al-FÔN-zēn)	g.	Time for annual communion
8.	Parliament	h.	City French popes preferred to Rome
9.	Parlement of Paris (PAR-le-mon)	i.	Production by a series of specialized off-site workers
10.	Golden Horde	j.	The sin of charging interest on a loan
11.	Russian Mesopotamia	k.	Highest court in France until 1789
12.	tsar (zar)	l.	Long-term partnership
13.	Avignon (a-vē-NYON)	m.	Organizations of merchants and master artisans
14.	Beguines (BEG-ēn)	n.	Star chart used in navigation
15.	Corpus Christi Day (KRIS-tē)	o.	A boy or girl being trained for a guild-regulated job

SIGNIFICANT INDIVIDUALS

1. Henry III

2. Simon de Montfort
(SĒ-mon deh mon-FOR)

3. Edward I

4. Philip IV, the Fair

5. Rudolf Habsburg (HAPS-burg)

6. Michael VIII Palaeologus
(pā-lē-OL-o-gus)

7. Genghis Khan (JEN-giz KAN)

8. Ivan I

9. Ivan III

10. Boniface VIII

11. Clement V

12. Catherine of Siena (sē-EN-a)

13. St. Bonaventure
(bon-a-ven-TYOOR)

14. Roger Bacon

15. William of Ockham (OK-am)

16. Dante (don-TĀ)

a. Mongol who created world's largest empire (1206-1227)

b. First emperor of the dynasty that would rule the Holy Roman Empire last and longest (r.1273-1291)

c. First prominent Muscovite prince (r.1328-1341)

d. Author of *Divine Comedy*

e. Pope whose bluff was called (r.1294-1303)

f. Saint famous for working with the poor and the sick (1347-1380)

g. English king who faced tax revolt (r.1216-1972)

h. First Avignon pope (r.1305-1314)

i. Philosopher and mystic (1221-1274)

j. Advocate of experimental science (1214-1294)

k. First emperor of Russia (r.1462-1505)

l. Unscrupulous French king (r.1285-1314)

m. Emperor who restored the Byzantine Empire (r.1261-1282)

n. French nobleman who led English rebellion (1208?-1265)

o. Philosopher who said simpler is better (ca.1285-ca.1349)

p. English king who conquered Wales (r.1272-1307)

CHRONOLOGICAL DIAGRAM

Late Middle Ages

Avignon Exile

1223	1261	1301	1321	1356	1480
		Model Parliament	Supression of the Templars	Catharine of Siena	
Mongols Enter Eastern Europe	Byzantines Recapture Constantinople	*Unam Sanctam*	*Divine Comedy*	Golden Bull	Standoff at Okra River

MAP EXERCISE

1.   Label the main political divisions of Europe around 1250.

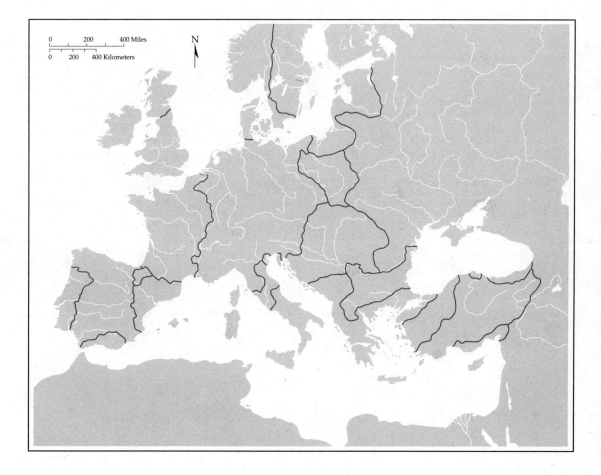

1. Show the movement of the East Slavs as the Principality of Kiev collapsed.

2. Indicate the nuclear area of Muscovy in 1325

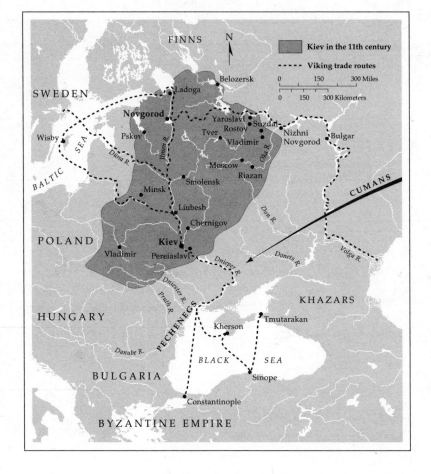

1. Label the territories of the Mongols, the Turks, Islam, Byzantium, the Holy Roman Empire, the kingdoms of England and France, and Christian kingdoms of Iberia around 1350.

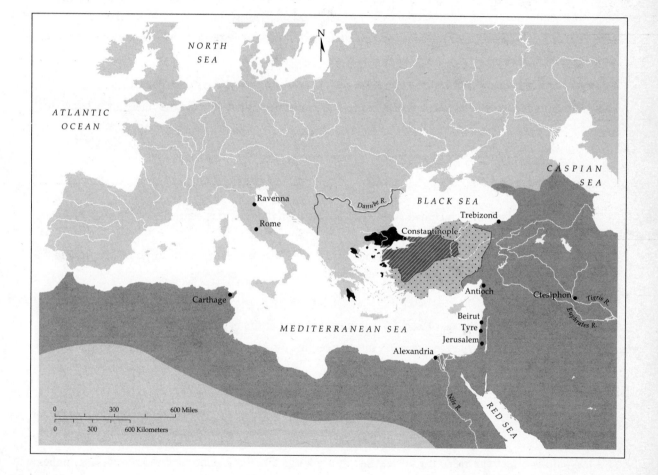

PROBLEMS FOR ANALYSIS

I. Cities, Trade, and Commerce

1. What advantages did independent towns have over those ruled by aristocratic landlords?

2. It can be argued that industry and commerce acquired many modern characteristics by the thirteenth century. Considering methods of manufacturing, the guilds, business institutions, and views toward economic life, do you agree? Why?

3. What were the attractions of living in a Medieval city? What were the disadvantages? Why, on balance, did cities draw people in?

II. Monarchies and the Development of Representative Institutions

1. Considering institutions such as Parliament, the Parlement of Paris, and the Cortes, should the thirteenth century be regarded politically as a period of representative assemblies? Why?

2. What special features of the Medieval English government were responsible for the enduring role of Parliament?

III. Government in the East

1. Why did Moscow become the center of the Russian state? What role did the relations between the Mongols and the prince of Moscow play in this?

2. On what basis should Ivan III be considered the founder of the modern Russian state? What policies did he pursue to this end?

IV. The Papacy and the Church

1. Why did the Papacy, which had seemed so powerful in the previous centuries, have such problems by the end of the thirteenth century?

2. Considering the issues that engaged pious lay people, why was there an upsurge of lay piety in the thirteenth and early fourteenth centuries?

V. Learning and Literature

1. What issues and methods of Scholasticism contributed to the beginnings of modern science?

2. In what ways does Dante's *Comedy* summarize the culture of this age? Compare the *Comedy* of Dante with the *Summa Theologica* of Aquinas.

SPECULATIONS

1. Would you have liked to live in a Medieval city? Would it have been preferable to living on the land?

2. Would you recommend to the thirteenth-century kings that they support representative assemblies or fight against them? Why?

3. At times, it appeared that the Mongols might sweep through Europe. Suppose that happened. How do you think it might have changed the development of Europe?

TRANSITIONS

"The Flowering of Medieval Civilization" examined the civilization of the Middle Ages in the West at a time of tremendous development that lay the foundations for further advances.

"The Urban Economy and the Consolidation of States" focuses first on the growth of towns and cities in response to the growth of manufacturing and trade. It goes on to describe the development of representative institutions in the kingdoms of the West, the recovery of Byzantium and the rise of Muscovy in the East, and the declining fortunes of the Papacy. The chapter finishes by discussing the rise of lay piety and mysticism, the first stirrings of science, and the monumental synthesis of Medieval civilization in Dante's *Divine Comedy*.

In "The West in Transition: Economy and Institutions," we will see a disaster of almost unimaginable magnitude hit Western Europe, and learn how European civilization struggled to cope with it during the late fourteenth and fifteenth centuries.

ANSWERS

Self Test

1b; 2c; 3b; 4c; 5b; 6b; 7c; 8b; 9c; 10b; 11d; 12c; 13c; 14c; 15b; 16b; 17d; 18a

Guide to Documents

I-1b; II-1a; III-1c

Significant Individuals

1g; 2n; 3p; 4l; 5b; 6m; 7a; 8c; 9k; 10e; 11h; 12f; 13i; 14j; 15o; 16d

Identification

1i; 2m; 3o; 4j; 5a; 6l; 7n; 8b; 9k; 10c; 11f; 12d; 13h; 14e; 15g

CHRONOLOGICAL DIAGRAM

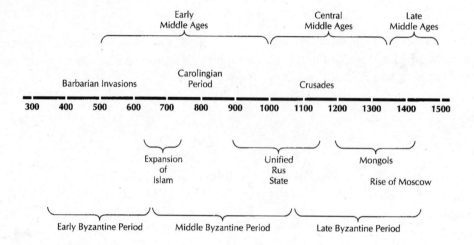

MAP EXERCISES

1. Indicate the following:

   a. Areas controlled by the Byzantine Empire at the end of Justianian's reign, after the Muslim conquests, after the Battle of Mazikert, and after the First Crusade. Give a date for each.

   b. Areas controlled by Islam at its maximum point of westward expansion. Indicate the approximate date.

   c. Areas controlled by Charlemagne. Indicate the approximate date.

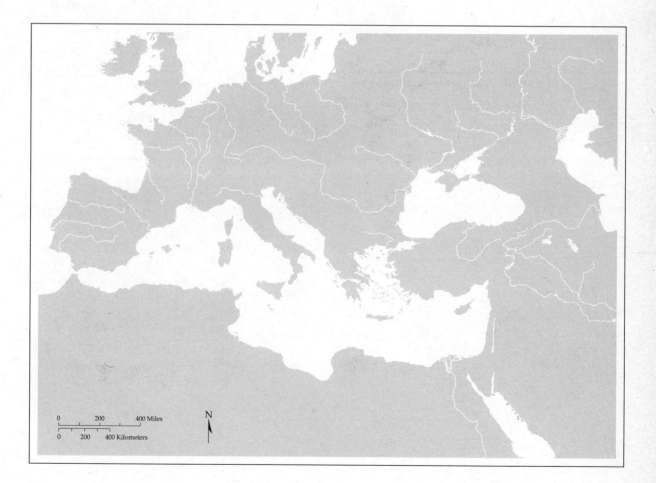

1. Indicate the crusader kingdoms and their approximate dates.
2. Indicate the political division of Europe around 1250.

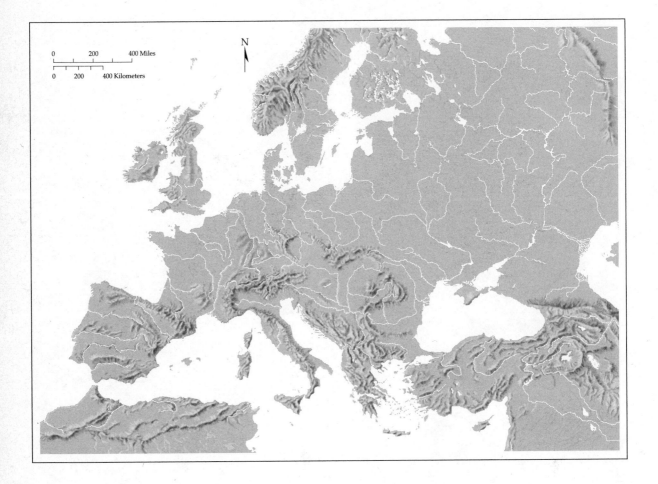

1. Indicate the areas controlled by the early Rus state (Kiev). Indicate the approximate date.

2. Indicate approximate areas controlled by the Mongols around 1300.

3. Indicate the Russian state in 1462.

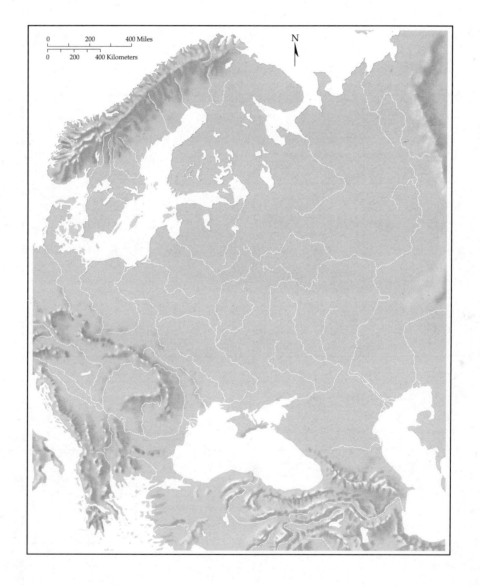

BOX CHART

Reproduce the Box Chart in a larger format in your notebook or on a separate sheet of paper. It is suggested that you devote one page for each column (i.e., chart all seven themes for each period or civilization on a separate page).

For a fuller explanation of the themes and how best to find material, see Introduction.

Chart 1: Western Europe

Period / Themes	500- 800 A.D.	800-1000	1000-1150	1150-1250	1250-1350
Social Structure: Groups in Society					
Politics: Events and Structures					
Economics: Production and Distribution					
Family Gender Roles Daily Life					
War: Relationship to larger society					
Religion: Beliefs, Communities, Conflicts					
Cultural Expression: Formal and Popular					

Note that while the columns correspond roughly to the chapters, the chapters do not hold strictly to chronology.

Chart 2: The East

Civilization Themes	Early Byzantine Empire (to 600)	Mid-Byzantine Empire (to 1282)	Islam to c.1100	Kiev Rus	Muscovy (to 1500)
Social Structure: Groups in Society					
Politics: Events and Structures					
Economics: Production and Distribution					
Family Gender Roles Daily Life					
War: Relationship to larger society					
Religion: Beliefs, Communities, Conflicts					
Cultural Expression: Formal and Popular					

CULTURAL STYLES

1.   Compare the interiors shown on pages 183, 220, 290, and 291-2. In what ways do their differences exemplify the civilizations that created them. In what ways are they similar?

2.   Compare the building on page 288 with the one on page 321. What styles are they? What differences do you see between them? How do those difference affect the perceptions of the viewer?

3.   Compare the statues shown on page 159, 228, 230, and 200. How did the art of sculpture change between the first and the third? How did it change from the second to the fourth? What is the relationship between the first and the last?

4.   Compare the sculpture on page 289 with the one on page 292. How do they differ? In what ways do they reflect the cultural style that they were made in?

5.   Compare the mosaics on pages 161 and 180, the illustration on page 204, and the painting on page 340. Can you see the development from the former on the latter? What characteristics are maintained? In what ways are the pictures different? What do they show about the relationship of Russia to Byzantium?

6.   Compare the paintings on page 227, page 299, and page 313. What similarities do you see among them? What differences? Is there any evidence that Western European painting became significantly more sophisticated during the time from the first to the last?

ELEVEN
BREAKDOWN AND RENEWAL IN AN AGE OF PLAGUE

CHAPTER HIGHLIGHTS

1. Europeans suffered economic dislocations and demographic disasters in the fourteenth and fifteenth centuries.

2. Europe suffered from depressions in trade and industry, but then recovered.

3. Economic, psychological, and social factors led the lower classes in rural and urban areas to revolt, adding to the upheaval of the period.

4. Wars, weakening central authority, and questions about royal succession reflected the considerable political instability of the period.

5. After the thirteenth century, the Byzantine Empire declined until it was finally overwhelmed by the expanding Ottoman Empire in 1453.

CHAPTER OUTLINE

I. Population Catastrophes

1. Demographic Decline

2. Plague

II. Economic Depression and Recovery

1. Agriculture

2. Protectionism

3. Technological Advances

4. The Standard of Living

III. Popular Unrest

1. Rural Revolts

2. Urban Revolts

3. The Seeds of Discontent

IV. The Governments of Europe

1. Roots of Political Unrest

2. The Nobility and Factional Strife

3. England, France, and the Hundred Years' War

4. The Tides of Battle

5. Joan of Arc

6. The Effects of the Hundred Years' War

7. The States of Italy

V. The Fall of Byzantium and the Ottoman Empire

1. The Fall of Constantinople

2. The Ottoman Empire

SELF TEST

1. Between 1300 and 1450, famines and plague reduced the number of people in Europe by

    a. about 10%.

    b. about one in four.

    c. about 1/3.

    d. ONE HALF TO TWO THIRDS!

2. The plague had all of the following effects EXCEPT

    a. people afflicted by it bled profusely from the nose or got large tumors and purple spots all over their body.

    b. it swept through communities like fire through dry tinder.

    c. it caused people to shun the families of the sick and refugees from afflicted communities.

    d. it inspired European doctors to make major strides in medicine as they sought a cure for it.

3. The famines that afflicted fourteenth and fifteenth century Europe resulted from all of the following EXCEPT

    a. enclosure, which caused cropland to be used for sheep-raising.

    b. overpopulation, which caused people to depend on poor land.

    c. excessive rainfall, which caused crops to rot in the fields.

    d. lack of infrastructure, which meant that relief could not get to the starving.

4. The initial response of governments to the economic disruption following the Black Death was to

    a. subsidize technological innovation to adapt to the new reality of high wages.

    b. pass laws at the expense of the lower classes in order to bolster the upper classes.

    c. encourage merchants and aristocrats to accept the inevitability of the new situation.

    d. embark on foreign wars in order to take by force what could no longer be bought.

5. The labor shortage caused all of the following changes in the status of European peasants EXCEPT

    a. formerly enserfed peasants in England gained their freedom.

    b. formerly free peasants in Eastern Europe were enserfed.

    c. some elements of serfdom were reimposed on the peasants in France, Italy, and Western Germany.

    d. most, but not all, of the elements serfdom were abandoned in Catalonia

6. All of the following technological advances occurred in the period after the Black Death EXCEPT

    a. invention of the astrolabe.

    b. techniques for making deeper mines.

    c. more efficient methods of metalworking.

    d. the rise of clockmaking and printing industries.

7. By the late fifteenth century the standard of living was generally

    a. falling, because there were not enough people to do all the work that needed to be done.

    b. rising, because the labor shortage caused wage and price rises that benefited everyone substantially.

    c. falling, because the damage done by the famines, plagues, and wars could not be made good.

    d. rising, because the process of adapting to the economic dislocations resulted in greater efficiency.

8. Peasant revolts occurred after the Black Death because

    a. the peasants were so impoverished that they were desperate.

    b. the peasants were upset that their burdens were increasing rather than decreasing.

    c. the peasants saw that the upper classes were so depleted that this was their chance to be rid of them.

    d. the peasants wanted revenge because they blamed the aristocrats for the plague.

9. The Florentine workers who rebelled in 1378 wanted

    a. steady work, secure wages, and representation in government.

    b. control of the city's government and major industries.

    c. land that they could farm so they could leave the squalid city slums.

    d. to seize the wealth of the rich and distribute it to the poor.

10. Popular revolts generally failed because

    a. the rebels would fall out among themselves before they could achieve success.

    b. the rebels' violence would alienate the majority of people, who then welcomed the restoration of order.

    c. the upper classes would make agreements when in danger, but renounce them once the danger had passed.

    d. the majority of people were content with their lot and would refuse to support the rebels.

11. The roots of political unrest included all of the following EXCEPT

    a. dynastic instability caused by the high death rate, which increased succession disputes.

    b. religious disputes caused by the increased piety of the people, including kings and aristocrats.

    c. changes in warfare that made it more expensive, leading governments to increase taxes.

    d. constitutional struggles between kings and representative assemblies.

12. Nobles enjoyed all of the following privileges EXCEPT

    a. exemption from most taxes.

    b. immunity from judicial torture.

    c. hunting rights.

    d. guaranteed incomes.

13. The most important cause of the Hundred Years' War was

    a. Edward III's claim to the French crown.

    b. French harassment of English merchants.

    c. the status of England's territories in France.

    d. the English threat to Flanders' wool industry.

14. The course of the Hundred Years' War was influenced by all of the following EXCEPT

    a. the battlefield superiority of English archers.

    b. France's size and resources.

    c. the inability of either side to gain decisive advantage.

    d. the strength of a series French kings.

15. Joan of Arc's primary effect on the Hundred Years' War was

    a. the qualms English soldiers had about fighting a saint.

    b. the popular support she generated for the king.

    c. her use of witchcraft to defeat the English.

    d. her ability to formulate and execute a long term strategy.

16. The Hundred Years' War had all of the following effects EXCEPT

    a. established the English parliament's extensive rights to participate in government.

    b. established the French monarchy's right to collect taxes without consent of the Estates.

    c. reinforced England's insular character and maritime orientation by removing it from the continent.

    d. left France in a position to dominate the rest of Europe because of its wealth and standing army.

17. Which of the following was NOT a city-state in northern Italy

    a. Milan, a manufacturing center ruled by a despot.

    b. Venice, a trading center ruled by the leading families.

    c. Florence, a financial center ruled by a boss.

    d. Naples, an agricultural center ruled by a king.

18. The purpose of Cosimo de Medici's alliance system was to

    a. maintain peace through a balance of power.

    b. establish Florentine hegemony in Italy.

    c. cripple Venetian power once and for all.

    d. keep the French out of Italian politics.

19. The Fall of Constantinople

    a. opened the Balkans to Ottoman invasion.

    b. disrupted the flow of trade between East and West.

    c. provoked a sudden exodus of scholars to Italy.

    d. psychologically shocked the Christian world.

20. All of the following were true of the Ottoman Empire EXCEPT

    a. it conquered vast territories.

    b. it enjoyed great richness.

    c. it persecuted Christianity.

    d. it lasted over 500 years.

GUIDE TO DOCUMENTS

I. Boccaccio on the Black Death

1. This selection reveals all of the following were assumptions Medieval people had about disease EXCEPT

    a. the Lord caused it.

    b. filth could cause it.

    c. some illnesses are inherently fatal.

    d. proximity increased the chance of contracting it.

2. According to the passage, all of the following efforts were made to deal with the plague EXCEPT

    a. enforcing public sanitation.

    b. circulating of advice on health.

    c. administering of medications.

    d. burning the clothes of the sick.

2. What might be the consequences of these facts reported by Boccaccio?

II. The Trial of Joan of Arc

1. How does this passage help explain the power and influence of Joan of Arc?

    a. She led an exemplary life in conformity with the expectations of her time.

    b. She knew when to stand her ground and when to make expedient concessions.

    c. She exuded confidence that she was carrying out God's direct commands.

    d. She exhibited a knowledge of Christian doctrine astonishing for a poor peasant girl.

2. What does this reveal about legal methods during these times, particularly in these sorts of cases?

III. The Sultan Mehmet II

1. According to Richard Knolles' description, Mehmet II had all of the following positive traits EXCEPT

    a. a love of learning.

    b. bravery.

    c. constancy.

    d. an intolerance of injustice.

2. According to the passage, Mehmet II had all of the following negative traits EXCEPT

    a. deceitfulness.

    b. vanity.

    c. greed.

    d. fickleness.

3. What does this passage reveal about the mixture of Mediterranean cultures during the fifteenth century?

SIGNIFICANT INDIVIDUALS

1. Johannes Gutenberg
   (YŎ-han-es GOO-ten-berg)

2. Aldus Manutius
   (ma-NOO-shē-us)

3. Henry De Vick

4. Wat Tyler

5. Henry VII

6. Joan of Arc (ark)

7. Charles VII

8. Philip the Bold

9. Gian Galeazzo Visconti
   (JĒ-an ga-LĒ-as-ō vēs-KON-tē)

10. Cosimo de Medici
    (ko-SĒ-mō MED-a-chē)

11. Lorenzo the Magnificent

12. Osman (OZ-man)

13. Mehmet II (ME-met)

14. Suleiman II, the Magnificent
    (su-lā-MAHN)

a. Leader of rebellious English peasants (14th century)

b. First Tudor king and restorer of order to England (r.1458-1509)

c. Inventor of printing press (15th century)

d. Ambitious and effective Duke of Milan (r.1378-1402)

e. Florentine banker and populist city boss (1389-1464)

f. Peasant girl who saved France (ca.1412-1431))

g. First known clockmaker (14th century)

h. Founder of the Ottoman dynasty (r.1290-1326)

i. Florentine ruler famous as patron of the arts (r.1469-1492)

j. French king who won Hundred Years' War (r.1422-1461)

k. First Duke of Burgundy (r.1363-1414)

l. Ottoman who captured Constantinople (4.1451-1481)

m. Sultan who took empire to height of power (r.1520-1566)

n. Printer who developed Italic type from Carolingian minuscule

CHRONOLOGICAL DIAGRAM

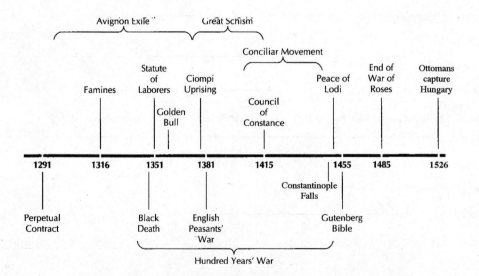

IDENTIFICATION

1. Black Death
2. Hanseatic League (han-sē-AT-ik)
3. enclosure
4. Statute of Laborers
5. English Peasants' War
6. Ciompi uprising (si-OM-pē)
7. Hundred Years' War
8. *gabelle* (ga-BEL)
9. *taille* (TA-y)
10. War of the Roses
11. Peace of Lodi (LŎ-dē)
12. Mohacs (MŎ-hach)
13. divan (DĬ-van)
14. vizier (vi-ZIR)
15. Janissaries

a. Alliance of north European trading cities
b. Foundation of Italian balance of power system
c. Ottoman chief administrator
d. Insurrection by poor urban workers
e. Civil war in England in late fifteenth century
f. Late fourteenth century insurrection in the countryside
g. Long war between France and England (1338-1453)
h. Ottoman council of advisors
i. Combination of bubonic and pneumonic plagues
j. Elite corps of Ottoman soldiers powerful in politics
k. Process of converting farmland into sheep pastures
l. English attempt to counteract law of supply and demand
m. Ottoman victory over Hungarians in 1526
n. Lucrative tax on salt
o. Direct tax, but not on nobles and clergy

MAP EXERCISES

1.   Label the five major states of Italy in 1454.

1. Indicate areas controlled by France, Burgundy, and England in 1339, in 1429, and in 1500.

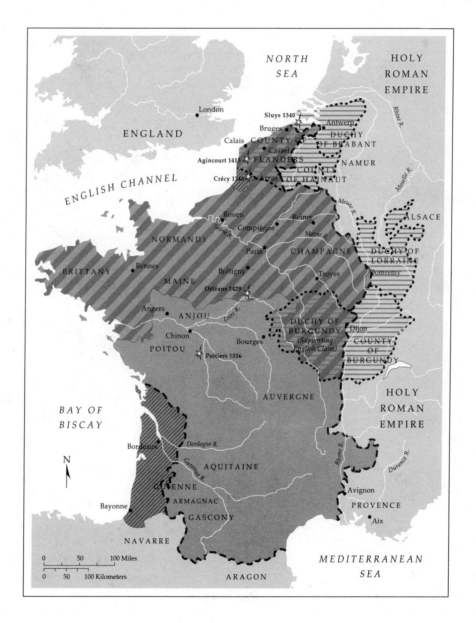

1.   Indicate the expansion of the Ottoman Empire between 1300 and 1566.

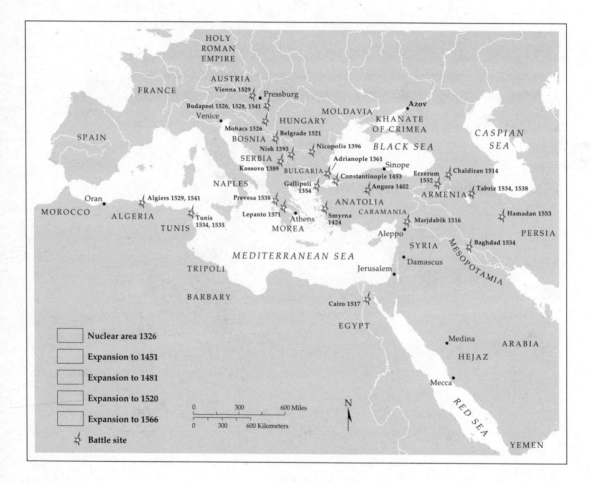

PROBLEMS FOR ANALYSIS

I. Population Catastrophes

1. What were the main developments that characterized the economic and demographic disasters of the fourteenth and fifteenth centuries? How can these developments best be explained?

II. Economic Depression and Recovery

1. Considering the loss of population, the technical advances, and the innovations in business institutions, was the long-term effect of the depression and demographic decline economically beneficial? Why?

2. What are the major issues in the history of women during the Middle Ages? Which do you think are the most important? Why?

III. Popular Unrest

1. What caused the rural and urban revolts of the fourteenth century? Analyze the governmental policies, the economic circumstances, and the psychological tensions that led to them.

IV. The Governments of Europe

1. In what ways was the feudal equilibrium in government broken in the fourteenth century? How is this illustrated by the Hundred Years' War?

2. Compare political development in Italy with that in France or England.

3. In what ways were the states of Italy able to gain relative stability during the fifteenth century?

V. The Fall of Byzantium and the Ottoman Empire

1. In what ways did the decline of Byzantium lead to important changes in the Mediterranean and the West?

2. How did the various Ottoman institutions contribute to the successful rise and expansion of this powerful empire? What role did the sultan and the Janissaries play?

SPECULATIONS

1. What do you think it would have been like to be a survivor of the plague? Discuss the different ways in which the experience would affect you materially and emotionally.

2. If a series of plagues and famines struck this country today, how do you think the people would react? What would the consequences be? Do you think there would be an experience parallel to that in fourteenth-century Europe? Why?

3. If England had been more successful militarily in the Hundred Years' Wars, do you think it might have maintained control over much of France for a long time? Why?

4. At times, it appeared that the Ottoman Turks might sweep through Europe. Suppose that happened. How do you think it might have changed the development of Europe?

TRANSITIONS

In "The Urban Economy and the Consolidation of States," the Medieval commercial economy, town life, and political development reached a high point, even as the problems of the papacy began to multiply.

In "Breakdown and Renewal in an Age of Plague" it was seen that Europe suffered a temporary decline. Compared with the thirteenth century, population decreased, political instability spread, and wars proliferated. Yet Europe had recovered and gained new dynamism by the second half of the fifteenth century. The period between the middle of the fourteenth and the fifteenth centuries should be considered both an autumn and a renaissance for Europe.

In "Tradition and Change in European Culture, 1300-1500," the culture, values, and society of that same period will be examined.

ANSWERS

Self Test

1d; 2d; 3a; 4b; 5d; 6a; 7d; 8b; 9a; 10c; 11b; 12d; 13c; 14d; 15b; 16d; 17d; 18a; 19d; 20c

Guide to Documents

I-1a; I-2d; II-1c; III-1c; III-2b

Significant Individuals

1c; 2n; 3g; 4a; 5b; 6f; 7j; 8k; 9d; 10e; 11i; 12h; 13l; 14m

Identification

1i; 2a; 3k; 4l; 5f; 6d; 7g; 8n; 9o; 10e; 11b; 12m; 13h; 14c; 15j

TWELVE
TRADITION AND CHANGE IN EUROPEAN CULTURE
1300-1500

CHAPTER HIGHLIGHTS

1. The culture of the Renaissance was pioneered by Italian scholars and artists.

2. Humanism was at the core of Renaissance culture.

3. The visual arts came to most vividly represent Humanism. Art and artists gained a new status among the elite.

4. In the last quarter of the fifteenth century Humanism came to the north, where the culture of the times emphasized chivalry, the cult of decay, and piety.

5. The papacy suffered a major schism and growing unpopularity. It was able to overcome its institutional weakness, but its unpopularity and the steady rise of lay piety and mysticism contributed to the renewal of open dissent.

OUTLINE AND SUMMARY

I. The New Learning

1. Humanism

2. Humanism in the Fifteenth Century

3. The Florentine Neoplatonists

4. The Heritage of Humanism

II. Art and Artists in the Italian Renaissance

1. Three Friends

2. The High Renaissance

3. Status and Perception

III. The Culture of the North

1. Chivalry and Decay

2. Contemporary Views of Northern Society

3. Art and Music

IV. Scholastic Philosophy, Religious Thought, and Piety

1. The "Modern Way"

2. Social and Scientific Thought

V. The State of Christendom

1. The Church

2. The Revival of the Papacy

3. Styles of Piety

4. Movements of Doctrinal Reform

SELF TEST

1. Humanism emphasized all of the following EXCEPT

    a. reading Classical writings in the original Latin and Greek.

    b. developing the ability to speak and write eloquently.

    c. rejecting religious rituals, institutions, and beliefs.

    d. pursuing perfection through moral philosophy.

2. Petrarch felt that the ultimate importance of studying the ancients was that it would enable people to

    a. write and speak in a more refined and eloquent way.

    b. escape from the misery of the present into an imagined past.

    c. imitate them, and thereby become more virtuous.

    d. understand the full richness and diversity of the human past.

3. Participation in public affairs was linked to early humanism by all of the following EXCEPT that

    a. humanists hoped to use government institutions to reform the masses.

    b. the purpose of rhetoric was to enable people to communicate better.

    c. Italian city-states were self-governing communities with lively politics.

    d. many of the ancients humanists admired had led active public lives.

4. As humanism spread, it had an impact as all of the following EXCEPT

    a. an educational system stressing knowledge useful for members of the social elite.

    b. a literary movement that reshaped the form and content of virtually all genres.

    c. a body of knowledge and manners that served to distinguish the upper classes.

    d. a political philosophy that caused the decline of despotism and rise of democracy.

5. The neoplatonists changed humanism by emphasizing all of the following EXCEPT

    a. the study of Greek.

    b. the philosophy of Plato.

    c. pursuit of personal perfection.

    d. the irreconcilablity of divergent truths.

6. The three friends who started the artistic revolution of the Renaissance include all EXCEPT

   a. Masaccio, the painter who emphasized nature, perspective, and classical models.

   b. Donatello, the sculptor who revived classical representation of the beauty of the human body.

   c. Brunelleschi, the architect who created the largest dome built in Europe since antiquity

   d. Leonardo, the multifaceted genius who painted masterpieces, studied nature, and built fortifications.

7. The High Renaissance

   a. was defined by a single man of overpowering genius, Leonardo da Vinci.

   b. saw the steady decline of the artistic trends begun the previous century.

   c. brought to a climax the artistic trends begun a century before.

   d. saw a shift in cultural initiative from artists to writers and philosophers.

8. The status of artists rose during the Renaissance because

   a. people were looking for a substitute for the clergy, whose reputation suffered because of their corruption.

   b. their works became status symbols for the upper classes, who sought distinction as patrons of the arts.

   c. they were drawn more and more from the upper classes, who needed new occupations as warfare declined.

   d. people felt that artists were gifted by God, and therefore patronage was a form of religious devotion.

9. Northern culture was characterized by all of the following EXCEPT

   a. a fascination with death, decay, and demons.

   b. the elaboration of chivalry and court culture.

   c. a commitment to the religious point of view.

   d. a rejection of Renaissance culture as impious.

10. Northern culture differed from Italian because

   a. the percentage of townspeople was far lower in the North.

   b. the plague was more severe in the North.

   c. malnutrition stunted Northerner's intellects.

   d. Northern society was highly urbanized.

11. Around 1500, northern Europe contained the chief center of

   a. architecture.

   b. music.

   c. painting.

   d. sculpture.

12. The chief change in late Medieval Scholasticism was

   a. a rejection of rational thought as a means of achieving useful knowledge.

   b. a renewed commitment to complete Aquinas' fusion of faith and reason.

   c. a focus on the way we describe things rather than on the reality of things.

   d. a growing skepticism that we can know anything about the material world.

13. Marsilius of Padua based his critique of Church power on

    a.   the nominalist position that reality is made up of discrete objects, not embracing universals.

    b.   the humanist position that people should cultivate their virtue in imitation of classical models.

    c.   Wycliff's criticism of the Church's remoteness from ordinary people and its dependence on Rome.

    d.   the Neoplatonist view that every being in the universe except God is impelled to seek perfection.

14. The popes responded to their financial problems with all of the following measures EXCEPT

    a.   collecting as a special tax one-third to one-half of an appointee's first year salary.

    b.   selling dispensations from the normal requirements of canon law.

    c.   selling indulgences, remissions of the temporal punishment for sin.

    d.   drastically reducing papal expenses by adopting a cult of virtuous poverty.

15. By end of the Great Schism

    a.   the papacy had regained its undisputed control of the Church.

    b.   the dominance of Church councils was firmly established.

    c.   the Trinity of three popes had come to be accepted.

    d.   everyone in Europe had been excommunicated.

16. The popes attempted to restore their power and prestige through all of the following EXCEPT

    a.   a magnificent building program in Rome.

    b.   patronage of artists and humanist scholars.

    c.   a vigorous military campaign to secure the Papal States.

    d.   a thoroughgoing reform of corrupt Church institutions.

17. Late Medieval mysticism emphasized

    a.   fasting, pilgrimages, and other ritual acts.

    b.   the interior experience of communion with God.

    c.   logical proofs of God's necessary existence.

    d.   rejection of the Church hierarchy and beliefs.

18. Lay piety involved all of the following EXCEPT

    a.   increased participation by women in religion.

    b.   an emphasis on charity and good works.

    c.   greater dependence on clerical intercession with God.

    d.   simplicity and humility in imitation of Christ.

19. Both Wycliff and Hus emphasized all of the following EXCEPT

    a.   the corruption of the Church.

    b.   the ultimate authority of the Bible.

    c.   the invalidity of the sacraments.

    d.   the community of all the faithful.

20. Humanism influenced religious dissent by

   a. emphasizing the superiority of original texts.

   b. pointing up the sinfulness of material concerns.

   c. refuting the Church's claims about transubstantiation.

   d. mobilizing the princes against Church power.

GUIDE TO DOCUMENTS

I. Petrarch on Ancient Rome

1. All of the following bothered Petrarch about people of his own time EXCEPT

   a. they were money grubbing.

   b. they wanted only physical pleasures.

   c. they were following the wrong religion.

   d. they were lawless and brutal.

2. What favorable characteristic of Roman times that he actually specifies in this passage is

   a. the way that people were able to be more moral.

   b. the great historical figures and historians who lived then.

   c. the religious devotion that people exhibited.

   d. the ease with which one could forget time and place then.

3. In what ways does Petrarch reflect the concerns of Italian Humanism?

II. Isabella d'Este's Quest for Art

1. What does this document reveal about patrons' motives for acquiring art during the Renaissance?

   a. They saw works of art more as investments than as aesthetic experiences.

   b. They valued contact with the artists more than the work the artists produced.

   c. They were more concerned about who the artist was than what painting was of.

   d. They cared more about the reputation of the artist than the quality of the painting.

2. What concerns and demands faced leading artists of the Renaissance such as Bellini and Leonardo da Vinci?

III. Hus at Constance

1. What point was of most concern to Hus in this passage?

   a. His honor is intact because he did not give in to threats or tricks.

   b. His views were not refuted through logic or reference to the Bible.

   c. The Council was made up of overly proud and avaricious men.

   d. The Czech nation has a special mission to rescue Christianity.

2. Why might Hus be considered so dangerous to Church authorities?

SIGNIFICANT INDIVIDUALS

1. Francesco Petrarch (PĒ-trark)

2. Giovanni Boccaccio
   (bō-ka-CHĒ-ō)

3. Baldassare Castiglione
   (kas-tē-LYŌ-nā)

4. Marsilio Ficino (fē-CHĒ-nō)

5. Pico della Mirandola
   (PĒ-kō DEL-la mē-RAN-dō-la)

6. Marsilius of Padua

7. Giotto (JOT-tō)

8. Masaccio (mah-SAHT-chō)

9. Jan Van Eyck (īk)

10. Raphael Santi (RAF-ē-al)

11. Leonardo da Vinci (VĒN-chē)

12. Michelangelo (mī-kel-AN-je-lō)

13. Albrecht Dürer (DEU-rer)

14. Martin V

15. Meister Eckhart
    (MĪ-ster Ek-hart)

16. Thomas à Kempis (ah KEM-pis)

17. John Wycliffe (WIK-lif)

18. Jan Hus

a. Neoplatonist translator and philosopher (1433-1499)

b. Widely known early Florentine artist (1276-1336)

c. Nominalist political philosopher (1290?-1343)

d. Pope, began revival of papacy and Rome (r.1417-1431)

e. First great painter in oils (1385-1440)

f. Student of Aquinas and mystic (1260?-1327)

g. Early humanist who wrote *The Decameron* (1313-1375)

h. English critic of the Church (1320?-1384)

i. Painter, scientist, and engineer (1452-1520)

j. Bohemian reformer betrayed at Constance (1369-1415)

k. Author who said emulate the life of Christ (1380-1471)

l. Painter who pioneered perspective (1401-1428)

m. Author of manual of behavior, *The Courtier* (1478-1529)

n. Painter with harmonious, serene style (1483-1520)

o. Thinker who claimed to be able to prove the unity of all philosophies (1463-1494)

p. Painter, sculptor, and architect (1475-1564)

q. Leading artist of the Northern Renaissance (1471-1528)

r. Most influential early humanist (1304-1374)

CHRONOLOGICAL DIAGRAM

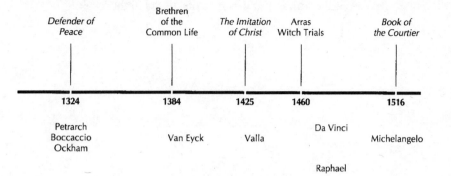

IDENTIFICATION

1. rhetoric (RET-o-rik)

2. civic Humanism

3. *Casa Giocosa* (KA-sa JŎ-ko-sa)

4. Neoplatonism

5. genius

6. Bretheren of the Common Life

7. *devotio moderna* (di-VŎT-ē-ō mō-DER-na)

8. nominalists

9. *via moderna* (VĒ-a mō-DER-na)

10. Great Schism

11. conciliar movement

12. Council of Constance

13. lay piety

14. confraternities

15. Lollards

16. Hussites

a. Desire of ordinary people for religious experience

b. Division of Church between two, and then three, popes

c. Style of lay piety imparted by followers of Gerhard Groote

d. Scholastics who focused on the way we describe the world

e. Education in methods of good speaking and writing

f. Bohemian religious rebels who won minor concessions

g. Religious guilds devoted to religious services and charity

h. School where humanist education developed furthest

i. Gathering that ended division of Church and burned Hus

j. Mystical and educational lay religious organization

k. Belief that participation in public affairs is part of full life

l. Followers of Wycliff

m. Special spirit Vasari said set certain artists apart

n. Humanist movement that emphasized contemplation

o. Drive to make Church councils superior to pope

p. Term used for Ockhamite philosophy

MAP EXERCISE

1.   Circle the main centers of the Italian Renaissance discussed in the book.

PROBLEMS FOR ANALYSIS

I. The New Learning

1. What are the main characteristics of Italian Humanism? How do these compare with earlier medieval Scholasticism? Why were Italian humanists so interested in Classical civilization?

II. Art and Artists in the Italian Renaissance

1. In what ways did art change in the Renaissance?
2. In what ways did the role of the artist and the prestige attached to art change? Why was this so important?
3. Compare Italian and northern art.

III. The Culture of the North

1. What social and historical factors help explain the differences between the culture of the north and the culture of Italy?
2. Is it fair to argue that the culture of the north was one of pessimism and decay, a holdover from the Middle Ages? Why?

IV. Scholastic Philosophy, Religious Thought, and Piety

1. Compare the analytical religious thought of nominalists, such as William of Ockham, with the synthetic Scholasticism of Thomas Aquinas.
2. In what ways were foundations for later scientific developments created in the fourteenth and fifteenth centuries?

V. The State of Christendom

1. Explain how the Avignon exile, the Great Schism, and the conciliar movement contributed to the weakening of the Church and, especially, papal authority. How did the papacy's secular concerns contribute to this?
2. Was mystical piety a rejection of the teachings of the medieval Church?
3. Why do you think that in both philosophy and religion movements that identified themselves as "modern" appeared during this period? What was going on in European civilization that made this distinction meaningful at this point in history?

SPECULATIONS

1. The fourteenth and fifteenth centuries have been described as a period of political, economic, and social turmoil and disaster. Yet, it was also a period of extraordinary cultural creativity. How can you explain this apparent contradiction?
2. Considering his designs for the airplane, tank, and submarine, should Leonardo da Vinci be considered as important as an inventor as he was an artist? Why?
3. How do you imagine a noble from one of the northern courts would react upon visiting Florence in the mid-fourteenth century? Why?
4. Suppose you were one of the popes during the Great Schism. How would you explain the Great Schism, and what policies would you follow? Why?

TRANSITIONS

In "Breakdown and Renewal in an Age of Plague," the economic depression, social disasters, and political instability of the fourteenth and fifteenth centuries were examined. The picture at that period was gloomy compared to the thirteenth century.

In "Tradition and Change in Europe Culture, 1300-1500," we see that the same period was also one of extraordinary cultural creativity. In Italy a humanistic and artistic culture, responding to the new patronage of the well-to-do literate laity, grew. In the north, a more conservative culture evolved, influenced by Italian developments, but retaining the ideals of chivalry and a strong commitment to Christian religiosity. The latter combined with dismay about clerical corruption to produce the appearance of radical dissent.

In "Reformations in Religion," the great religious upheavals that destroyed religious unity in the West will be analyzed.

ANSWERS

Self Test

1c; 2c; 3a; 4d; 5d; 6d; 7c; 8b; 9d; 10a; 11b; 12c; 13a; 14d; 15d; 16d; 17b; 18c; 19c; 20a

Guide to Documents

I-1c; I-2b; II-1c; III-1b

Significant Individuals

1r; 2g; 3m; 4a; 5o; 6c; 7b; 8l; 9e; 10n; 11i; 12p; 13q; 14d; 15f; 16k; 17h; 18j

Identification

1e; 2k; 3h; 4n; 5m; 6j; 7c; 8d; 9p; 10b; 11o; 12i; 13a; 14g; 15l; 16f

CHAPTER HIGHLIGHTS

1. Discontent with the Church and a growing demand for spiritual consolation combined to set the stage for the Reformation. Northern humanists combined themes of Italian Humanism with religious concerns, creating an intellectual environment for the Reformation.

2. Lutheranism, based upon the doctrine of justification by faith and the idea that the Bible was the sole religious authority, grew within the politically divided Holy Roman Empire.

3. Zwingli and Calvin led new reform movements, and other groups, such as the Anabaptists and the Melchiorites, led more radical breaks from established religion.

4. Led by Pope Paul III, the Council of Trent, and the Jesuits, the Catholic Church reformed itself and initiated a revival of Catholicism.

CHAPTER OUTLINE

I. Piety and Dissent

1. Doctrine and Reform

2. Causes of Discontent

3. Popular Religion

4. Piety and Protest in Literature and Art

5. Christian Humanism

II. The Lutheran Reformation

1. The Conditions for Change

2. Martin Luther

3. The Break with Rome

4. Lutheran Doctrine and Practice

5. The Spread of Lutheranism

6. Disorder and Revolt

7. Lutheranism Established

III. The Spread of Protestantism

1. Zwingli and the Radicals

2. Persecution

3. John Calvin

4. Calvinism

5. The Anglican Church

IV. The Catholic Revival

1. Strengths and Weaknesses

2. The Council of Trent

3. The Aftermath of Trent

4. Ignatius Loyola

5. The Jesuits

6. Religion and Politics

SELF TEST

1. The two traditions about how a sinful human beings can gain salvation are

    a. (1) Church ritual and (2) good works.

    b. (1) Good works and (2) clerical intercession.

    c. (1) Church ritual and (2) individual faith.

    d. (1) Individual faith and (2) love of God

2. In the late Medieval period, lay people sought a more personal religious experience through all EXCEPT

    a. reading the Bible and early Church fathers.

    b. joining religious orders in unprecedented numbers.

    c. establishing lay fraternities for worship and charity.

    d. destroying cosmetics, dice, and other frivolities.

3. All of the following eroded the prestige of the late Medieval papacy EXCEPT

    a. its confusion during the Avignon and Schism periods.

    b. its focus on worldly concerns like power politics.

    c. its fiscal expedients and extravagent spending.

    d. the successes of the Ottoman Turks.

4. New religious ideas were spread in all of the following ways EXCEPT

    a. sermons by the clergy.

    b. nightly village gatherings.

    c. printed books and broadsides.

    d. works of literature and art.

5. The Christian Humanists attempted to use humanistic techniques in the service of religion by

    a. fusing Neoplatonist philosophy with the Christian religion.

    b. retranslating and reanalyzing the Bible to understand it more accurately.

    c. refuting nominalism by drawing on ancient authorities.

    d. showing the parallel between civic Humanism and Christian "good works."

6. The Holy Roman Empire was ripe for Reformation for all of the following reasons EXCEPT

   a. in territories ruled by the Church, secular complaints exascerbated spirtual ones.

   b. its small governments could not resist papal exactions as national monarchs did.

   c. its rulers coveted the Church's wealth and property.

   d. the Holy Roman Emperor wanted to gain independence from the pope.

7. Martin Luther's basic problem was that

   a. he was unhappy in the career track that he had chosen.

   b. he identified the pope with his father.

   c. he felt a righteous God would never forgive his sins.

   d. he felt unworthy to perform the sacraments.

8. The pope excommunicated Luther because

   a. he disputed the legitimacy of indulgences in the 95 Theses.

   b. he rejected the pope's authority and the validity of the sacraments.

   c. he refused to recant his beliefs at the Diet of Worms.

   d. he defied an Imperial edict by accepting protection in Saxony.

9. Luther's last major act of reform was to

   a. define the doctrine of consubstantiation to make clear his rejection of transubstantiation.

   b. translate the Bible into German so ordinary people could read it for themselves.

   c. organize the Duke of Saxony's church, which became a model for Lutherans elsewhere.

   d. meet with Zwingli in an attempt to reconcile their interpretations of Christianity.

10. Popular enthusiasm for Luther's revolt was demonstrated by all of the following EXCEPT

    a. other preachers and phamphlets criticizing the Church proved a strong draw all over the Empire.

    b. there were waves of image smashing, reports of priests marrying, and efforts to simplify the sacraments.

    c. congregations all over the Empire and in neighboring countries began following Luther's teachings.

    d. radical preachers began calling for Lutheranism to be institutionalized as the Empire's state church.

11. All of the following groups invoked Luther's ideas to justify taking up arms EXCEPT

    a. the Swiss cantons.

    b. the Imperial knights.

    c. the peasantry.

    d. the Protestant princes.

12. Luther's doctrine of the equality of all believers in the eyes of God had all of the following effects EXCEPT

    a. it justified antimonarchical constitutional theories.

    b. it originated independent and pioneering behavior among Europeans.

    c. it allowed people to feel that all occupations were equally worthy.

    d. it undermined the hierarchic view of the universe.

13. Zwingli and Luther were unable to resolve their differences on

    a. who would be the new religion's ultimate leader.

    b. exactly what happens during communion.

    c. how much religious leaders should supervise daily life.

    d. the validity of other reformers besides themselves.

14. The Melchiorite Anabaptists at Münster did all of the following EXCEPT

    a. forcibly rebaptized all citizens.

    b. burned all books but the Bible.

    c. abolished private property.

    d. instituted polygamy.

15. Calvinism was well adapted to struggle against Catholicism for all the following reasons EXCEPT

    a. its doctrine of predestination instilled firm confidence in its adherents.

    b. it had a disciplined, hierarchical organization that defined clearly each member's position.

    c. its tenets were left vague, so different congregations could adapt them to local conditions.

    d. it had a secure base at Geneva from which to disseminate missionaries propaganda.

16. Henry VIII separated the English Church from Rome

    a. because of the strength of Lutheranism among his subjects.

    b. because he was moved by Luther's message.

    c. in order to cement an alliance with the Emperor.

    d. to get a divorce.

17. The pre-existing strengths of the Catholic Church included all of the following EXCEPT

    a. venerable traditions and splendid ceremonies.

    b. phenomenal wealth.

    c. clearly defined doctrines.

    d. Paul III.

18. The Council of Trent accomplished all of the following EXCEPT

    a. clearly reaffirming doctrines challenged by the Protestants.

    b. establishing the outward, sacramental orientation of the Church.

    c. strengthening the power of the pope.

    d. updating the version of the Bible accepted as authoritative.

19. The most common contribution of women to the Counter-Reformation was

    a. as mystics.

    b. through charitable activities.

    c. by affecting their husbands' faith.

    d. by founding new orders.

20. The core element of Ignatius Loyola's new order was

    a. strictly enforced military discipline.

    b. carefully structured spiritual experiences.

    c. rigorous educational preparation.

    d. flexibilty when courting wavering rulers.

21. All of the following were principal functions of the Society of Jesus EXCEPT

    a. hearing confessions.

    b. teaching.

    c. writing scholarly works.

    d. performing missionary work.

GUIDE TO DOCUMENTS

I. Luther's "Experience in the Tower"

1. In light of this document, "justification by faith" meant to Luther that

    a. God's existence is proved by faith.

    b. one secures forgiveness for sin and a righteous life by believing in God.

    c. a person obtains forgiveness for sin and leads a righteous life as a gift from God.

    d. a believer is reborn when he or she obtains faith.

2. Why might an experience like this be so crucial to someone like Luther?

II. The Trial of Elizabeth Dirks

1. In this passage Elizabeth Dirks rejects rituals and doctrines of the Roman Catholic Church because

    a. she rejects all patriarchal authority.

    b. she has never seen them work in practice.

    c. she accepts only what she has read in the Bible.

    d. she accepts only the revealled to her in mystical experiences.

2. Why were her beliefs viewed as threatening to the Roman Catholic Church?

3. What does this excerpt reveal about the beliefs that led Elizabeth Dirks and perhaps others to join radical groups during the Reformation?

III. St. Teresa's Visions

1. What does this excerpt reveal about the relationship between spirit and the physical world in St. Teresa's experience?

    a. spirit can alter the physical, as when the arrow pierces her heart.

    b. physical attractiveness is irrelevant in spiritual matters.

    c. spiritual experiences cannot be expressed in physical terms.

    d. spiritual perfection is expressed through physical beauty.

2. Why might some readers of the autobiography of St. Teresa find these passages so inspiring?

SIGNIFICANT INDIVIDUALS

1. Savonarola (sah-VON-a-rola)

2. Hieronymus Bosch
    (hï-e-RON-e-mus bos)

3. Peter Brueghel (BROI-gel))

4. Francois Rabelais (RAB-e-lā)

5. Desiderius Erasmus
    (i-RAZ-mus)

6. Thomas More

7. Martin Luther

8. Ulrich Zwingli
    (UL-rik TSVING-lē)

9. John Calvin

10. Thomas Cromwell

11. Julius II

12. Paul III

13. Ignatius Loyola
    (ig-NĂ-shē-us loi-Ŏ-la)

14. Francis Xavier (ZĂ-vē-er)

a. Monk who started Protestant Reformation (1483-1546)

b. Founder of militant Catholic order (1491-1556)

c. Radical Florentine religious reformer (1452-1498)

d. Early Swiss reformer (1484-1531)

e. Minister who figured out how to get Henry VIII his divorce (r.1509-1547)

f. Humanist, statesman, and author of *Utopia* (1478-1535)

g. the "Warrior Pope" (r. 1503-1513)

h. Author who called Church a mockery (1494?-1553)

i. Pope who galvinized the Church (1468-1549)

j. Painter of scenes from village life (1520?-1569)

k. Jesuit missionary to Japan (1506-1564)

l. Painter of fantastic, demonic scenes (1450-1516)

m. Learned Christian humanist who praised folly (1466?-1536)

n. Reformer who emphasized predestination (1509-1564)

CHRONOLOGICAL DIAGRAM

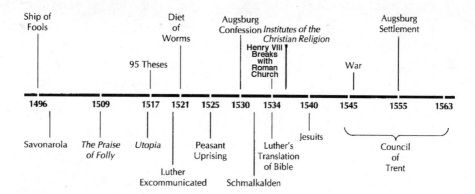

IDENTIFICATION

1. anticlerical

2. *veillée*

3. moveable type

4. *Utopia* (Ü-tö-pë-a)

5. "philosophy of Christ"

6. justification by faith

7. indulgences

8. 95 theses

9. Diet of Worms

10. priesthood of all believers

11. consubstantiation (Kon-sub-stan-shë-Ä-shun)

12. Augsburg Confession

13. Melchiorites (MEL-kê-or-ït)

14. predestination

15. Council of Trent

16. Jesuits (JEZH-oo-it)

17. Index of Forbidden Books

18. good works

a. Imaginary perfect society

b. Belief that all Christians are equal in eyes of God

c. Luther's challenge to indulgence peddlers

d. Official statement of Lutheranism

e. Belief that God predetermined who's saved and who's not

f. Nightly village gathering

g. Gathering where Luther refused to recant

h. Gathering that finally addressed Church's problems

i. Catholic reading list, not

j. Critical of the priesthood

k. Innovation that made practical the mass production of books

l. Dispensations from time in purgatory sold by Church

m. Belief that salvation comes from belief in God

n. Shock troops of the Counter Reformation

o. Christianity based on Christ's example and teachings

p. Doctrine that something can be two things at once

q. Deeds that help with salvation

r. Radical Protestants Lutherans and Catholics massacred

MAP EXERCISE

1.   Indicate the main Lutheran, Calvinist, and Anglican areas in the late 1500s.

PROBLEMS FOR ANALYSIS

I. Piety and Dissent

1.   What were the sources of religious discontent that preceded the Reformation? What evidence is there for this?

2.   Compare northern and Italian Humanism.

3.   In what ways is it appropriate to focus on Thomas More and Erasmus as representatives of northern Humanism?

II. The Lutheran Reformation

1.   What emotional needs motivated Luther? Why did his personal answers strike such a strong chord in others?

2.   What were the main differences in doctrine and practice between Catholicism and Lutheranism?

3.   "Despite his revolutionary actions, Martin Luther was quite authoritarian and conservative." Do you agree? Explain.

III. The Growth of Protestantism

1.   "Protestantism was not simply a single movement away from the Roman Catholic Church; it was a series of separate and often conflicting movements." Do you agree? Explain.

2.   Why did Calvinism develop into the most dynamic of the Protestant forces during the mid-sixteenth century?

IV. The Catholic Revival

1.   In what ways was the Catholic revival of the sixteenth century a Counter Reformation? In what ways was it a Catholic Reformation?

2.   How did Pope Paul III, the Council of Trent, and the Jesuits contribute to the Catholic revival?

3.   What emotional needs in people did Catholicism fulfill better than Protestantism?

SPECULATIONS

1.   Suppose you were the pope in 1515 but had the hindsight of a historian living in the 1990s. What might you have done to prevent the Reformation? Do you think your efforts would have had a good chance of succeeding?

2.   How important was Martin Luther to the Reformation? Do you think the Reformation would have occurred without him?

3.   Which do you think was more compatible with the Renaissance and the secular developments of the early sixteenth century, Catholicism or Protestantism? Explain.

TRANSITIONS

In "The West in Transition: Society and Culture," the dynamic cultural developments of the fourteenth and fifteenth centuries and the social conditions supporting those developments were examined.

In "Reformations in Religion," the shattering of religious unity in Europe during the first half of the sixteenth century is analyzed. The fundamental religious issue of the Reformation was how sinful humans could gain salvation. Increasingly, the Catholic Church answered this question by emphasizing the role of the Church. Reformers reversed this trend by emphasizing the inward and personal approach. But spiritual conflict quickly evolved into fanatical attacks on all sides; moderation and tolerance failed almost everywhere.

In "Economic Expansion and a New Politics," Europe experiences a political, economic, and geographic revival characterized by the growth of monarchical power, commercial growth, and overseas expansion.

ANSWERS

Self Test

1c; 2b; 3d; 4a; 5b; 6d; 7c; 8b; 9b; 10d; 11a; 12b; 13b; 14a; 15c; 16d; 17c; 18d; 19b; 20b; 21c

Guide to Documents

I-1b; II-1c; III-1d

Significant Individuals

1c; 2l; 3j; 4h; 5m; 6f; 7a; 8d; 9n; 10e; 11g; 12i; 13b; 14k

Identification

1j; 2f; 3k; 4a; 5o; 6m; 7l; 8c; 9g; 10b; 11p; 12d; 13r; 14e; 15h; 16n; 17i; 18q

FOURTEEN
ECONOMIC EXPANSION AND A NEW POLITICS

CHAPTER HIGHLIGHTS

1. In the sixteenth century, Europe experienced population and economic growth. A series of social developments stemmed from these changes.

2. Europeans, led by the Portuguese and then by the Spaniards, expanded over the globe establishing empires over vast areas.

3. "New monarchs" in Western Europe increased their authority and power.

4. In parts of Eastern Europe and Italy, central authority was unable to overcome forces that favored small, relatively autonomous units.

5. Initiated in Italy, new theories and practices of diplomacy and statecraft, focusing on the realities of power, spread throughout Europe.

CHAPTER OUTLINE

I. Expansion at Home

1. Population Increase

2. Economic Growth

3. Social Change

II. Expansion Overseas

1. The Portuguese

2. The Spaniards

3. The First Colonial Empire

III. The Centralization of Political Power

1. The "New Monarchs"

2. Tudor England

3. Valois France

4. Louis XI and Charles VIII

5. Louis XII, Francis I, and Henri II

6. United Spain

7. Charles V, Holy Roman Emperor

IV. The Splintered States

1. The Holy Roman Empire

2. Eastern Europe

3. Italy

V. The New Statecraft

1. International Relations

2. Machiavelli and Guicciardini

SELF TEST

1. All of the following were true of Europe's population growth in the sixteenth century EXCEPT

    a. the overall population increased by approximately 50%.

    b. cities grew faster than the overall population.

    c. it made wheat five times more expensive.

    d. it caused the decline of the wool trade as pastures became cropland.

2. Europe's economic expansion was fueled by all of the following EXCEPT

    a. increased demand because of the increased population.

    b. huge imports of silver from America.

    c. increasing focus on accumulation of capital for its own sake.

    d. government's stabilizing influence on the financial markets.

3. Which of the following business concepts originated during this period?

    a. the business firm as an entity independent of its owner.

    b. payment of debts through notes rather than coin.

    c. the role of banks as repositories of savings and sources of loans.

    d. taking of great risks in hopes of great gains and reinvesting profits.

4. During the sixteenth century, all of the following followed from the commercial revolution EXCEPT

    a. large numbers of peasants lost their land and became beggars.

    b. destitute vagrants floated across the countryside and filled the towns.

    c. private charity was rapidly mobilized and proved sufficient to solve the problem.

    d. widespread poverty, crime, and disorder became chronic features of town and country life.

5. The most widely shared motivation behind the voyages of exploration and conquest was

    a. the desire to spread Christianity.

    b. the lure of riches.

    c. the desire to explore the unknown.

    d. the hope of finding a lost Christian land.

6. The Portuguese empire was all of the following EXCEPT

    a. based carrying goods by sea around Africa between Europe and the rich civilizations of the Indian Ocean.

    b. created and sustained by the superior fighting power of Portugal's cannon-armed ships.

    c. made up of small enclaves along the coasts in Africa and the Indian Ocean basin.

    d. welcomed by the South Asians as a new source of wealth that would benefit everyone.

7. The Spanish empire was all of the following EXCEPT

    a. based on extracting wealth by slave labor from America and shipping it to Europe.

    b. created and sustained by the Europeans' military superiority, ruthless ambition, and greater sophistication.

    c. made up of extensive territories on both the North and South American continents.

    d. established almost bloodlessly and maintained with minimal disruption of the Native Americans' lives.

8. The Europeans needed to bring Black African slaves to America because

    a. there were very few Native Americans to begin with.

    b. Africans were more docile workers than the Native Americans.

    c. the Europeans massacred most of the Native Americans when conquering them.

    d. millions of Native Americans died from disease and mistreatment after they were conquered.

9. Exploration and colonization brought all of the following benefits to Europe EXCEPT

    a. the Portuguese got the profits from trade between Europe and the East that had gone mainly to Muslims.

    b. the Spanish financed a century of predominance in Europe largely with American silver.

    c. the rest of Europe enjoyed plentiful currency, which facilitated economic growth.

    d. economic expansion alleviated the poverty of Europe's lower classes.

10. The most important "new" monarchs were rulers of all of the following EXCEPT

    a. Italy.

    b. England.

    c. France.

    d. Spain.

11. Henry VII and Henry VIII were similar in their

    a. greater interest in domestic than foreign affairs

    b. flamboyant, expansive personalities.

    c. desire to reform religion.

    d. inability to manage the affairs of the government.

12. At the end of the Hundred Years' War, the key to the French monarchy's power was its

    a. control over tax rates.

    b. standing army.

    c. streamlined administration.

    d. control over outlying provinces.

13. Louis XI's most notable achievement was

    a. the destruction of Burgundy.

    b. the invasion of Italy.

    c. getting control of major Church appointments.

    d. curbing expenditures on the army.

14. Which of the following Valois kings accomplished the most during his reign?

    a.   Charles VIII.

    b.   Louis XII.

    c.   Francis I.

    d.   Henri II.

15. Ferdinand and Isabella followed all of the following policies while uniting Spain EXCEPT

    a.   reducing the role of great nobles while recruiting the *hidalgos*, or lesser nobility, into their administration.

    b.   gaining control of appointments to high Church offices in territory taken from the Muslims.

    c.   using viceroys to create a uniform administration in all parts of the realm.

    d.   persecuting Jews and converted Muslims in order to gain popularity and authority.

16. The Holy Roman Emperor Charles V also ruled all of the following territories EXCEPT

    a.   Spain and its American empire.

    b.   much of Italy.

    c.   Sicily, Sardinia, and western Hungary.

    d.   France and England.

17. The main locus of power in the Holy Roman Empire was

    a.   the Emperor's court.

    b.   the Imperial Diet.

    c.   the princes.

    d.   the Imperial cities.

18. The nobles of Hungary did all of the following EXCEPT

    a.   refuse to finance the monarchy's standing army.

    b.   impose serfdom on the peasants.

    c.   give up their German lands to gain Habsburg support.

    d.   support the Ottoman Empire.

19. The Italian wars highlighted

    a.   the effectiveness of balance of power diplomacy.

    b.   the weakness of city-states relative to national states.

    c.   the Italians' military as well as economic and cultural superiority.

    d.   the flaws in the republican governments of Venice and Florence.

20. The essential innovation of Italian diplomacy was

    a.   the formal protocol of international relations.

    b.   the political analysis.

    c.   the resident ambassador.

    d.   diplomatic immunities.

21. Machiavelli's essential innovation was to focus on

    a.   the reasons why power does or should exist.

    b.   the practicalities of how power works.

    c.   the relationship of power to other practical activities like cooking.

    d.   the moral issues raised by the use of power.

GUIDE TO DOCUMENTS

Two Views of Columbus

1. S.E. Morison admires all of the following about Columbus EXCEPT

    a.   his appreciation of exotic beauty.

    b.   his religious faith.

    c.   the effects of his accomplishment.

    d.   his self-confidence.

2. Kirkpatrick Sale criticizes all of the following about Columbus EXCEPT

    a.   his bravery.

    b.   his seamanship.

    c.   his arrogance toward nature.

    d.   the effects of his accomplishment.

3. How do you explain the differences between these two views of Columbus? Which do you find more persuasive? Why?

Henry VIII Claims Independence from the Pope

1. Henry VIII asserts the judicial independence of his realm on all of the following bases EXCEPT?

    a.   historical accounts of England's undivided sovereignty .

    b.   God's mandate of whole and entire power to the king.

    c.   Roman Law's concept of the emperor's sovereign power.

    d.   the concurrence of King, Lords, and Commons.

2. Why might this legal question be of such great historical significance?

SIGNIFICANT INDIVIDUALS

1. Johannes Fugger (Foog-er)

2. Henry the Navigator

3. Vasco da Gama (GAM-a)

4. Christopher Columbus

5. Ferdinand Magellan (ma-JEL-an)

6. Hernando Cortés (kor-TEZ)

7. Francisco Pizzaro (pi-ZAH-rō)

8. Henry VII

9. Henry VIII

10. Louis XI

11. Francis I

12. Ferdinand and Isabella

13. Charles V

14. Matthias Corvinus (KOR-vĭn-us)

15. Niccolò Machiavelli (mah-kyah-VEL-ē)

16. Francesco Guicciardini (gwĕt-char-DĒ-nē)

a. Genoese who discovered America for Spain (1451-1506)

b. First Tudor king, established royal power (r.1485-1509)

c. French king known as "the Spider" (r. 1461-1483)

d. *Conquistador* who conquered Aztec Empire (1485-1547)

e. Portuguese prince behind much exploration (1394-1460)

f. Successful Hungarian king (r. 1458-1490)

g. Diplomat who wrote on realities of power (1469-1527)

h. French king who began appointing bishops (r.1515-1547)

i. Explorer whose expedition circled the globe (1480-1521)

j. Historian of Italy who used original sources (1483-1520)

k. Founder of German banking family (14th century)

l. *Conquistador* who conquered Incan Empire (1470?-1541)

m. Habsburg heir who ruled much of Europe (r.1516-1556)

n. Portuguese explorer who made it to India (1469?-1524)

o. King of Aragon (r.1479–1516) and Queen of Castile (r.1474–1504) who united Spain

p. Arrogant, dazzling English king (r.1509-1547)

CHRONOLOGICAL DIAGRAM

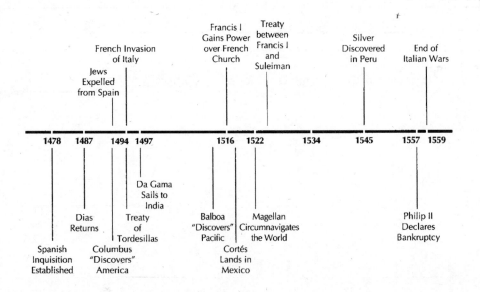

IDENTIFICATION

1. the commercial revolution
2. capitalism
3. viceroy
4. justice of the peace
5. the Star Chamber
6. estates
7. standing army
8. sale of offices
9. "new monarchs"
10. gentry
11. *hidalgo* (hi-DAL-gō)
12. Moriscos (mo-RIS-kō)
13. Diet
14. resident ambassador
15. balance of power
16. *The Prince*

a. Well-to-do English non-nobles who dominated localities
b. Representative of the crown in Spanish territories
c. 15th and 16th centuries reforming kings and queens
d. Outlook and behaviors emphasizing pursuit of profit
e. Permanent military force maintained by government
f. New mechanisms for organizing large-scale businesses
g. Lesser aristocracy who served Spanish crown
h. Representative assembly in Germany
i. Practical book describing how power works
j. Practice of selling government positions to raise money
k. International system in which no state can dominate rest
l. Representative assemblies in France
m. Royal councilors acting as court in England
n. Converted Jews and former Muslims in Spain
o. Local official in England recruited from gentry
p. Permanent representative of one state to another

MAP EXERCISES

1.   Label the *main* political divisions of Europe in the mid-sixteenth century.

2.   Indicate the areas ruled by Charles V.

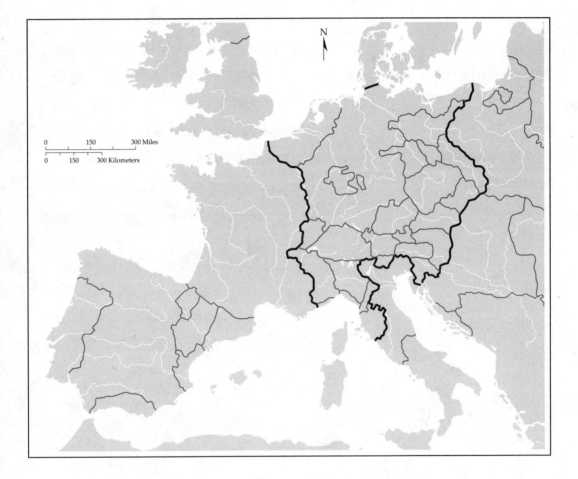

1. Label Portuguese possessions and Spanish possessions.

2. Indicate the routes taken by Columbus, Dias, da Gama, and Magellan and his crew.

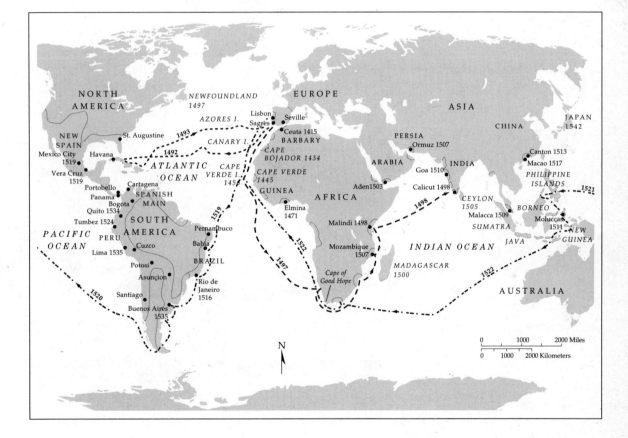

PROBLEMS FOR ANALYSIS

I. Expansion at Home

1. What were some of the economic and social consequences of population increase?
2. What developments in prices, commerce, and industry evidenced economic growth? Why? What were the consequences of this for the quality of life of the different social classes?

II. Expansion Overseas

1. What motivated exploration and expansion?
2. Distinguish between the Portuguese and Spanish patterns of exploration and expansion. What part did the size of Spain and of fifteenth- and sixteenth-century political and military developments play in this difference?
3. What were the costs of European exploration and expansion? Who bore them? What were the benefits? Who gained them?

III. The Centralization of Political Power

1. What developments and policies characterized the "new monarchies" of Western Europe?
2. Compare any two "new monarchies," focusing on the developments that distinguished the two, despite their similarities.

IV. The Splintered States

1. Who became the holders of power in Italy and much of Eastern Europe with the failure of central authority to grow ? What were the consequences for the lower classes?

V. The New Statecraft

1. What distinguished diplomacy during the sixteenth century from that of previous time? Why did Italy play such an important role in this?
2. Machiavelli and Guicciardini were original observers of contemporary political events. What was so importantly new about their observations? In what ways did their observations reflect the events of their times?

SPECULATIONS

1. If Machiavelli were alive today, what kinds of recommendations would he make to someone who wanted to gain and retain political office?
2. If you were adviser to Charles V, what policies would you suggest to retain the wealth coming from South America within Spain? What factors would you have to consider in making your recommendations?
3. Considering both the costs and benefits of European expansion, do you think on balance that it was a good thing? Is it possible that comparable benefits have been realized at less cost in the context of the times?
4. Contrast European expansion with that of some or all of the following: the Ottomans, the Mongols, the Arabs, the Romans, and the Greeks. Was the European case qualitatively different? Why or why not?

160

TRANSITIONS

In "Reformations in Religion," the religious revolutions that tore Europe apart during the sixteenth century were examined.

In "Economic Expansion and a New Politics," Europe experienced population and economic growth. Europe also expanded geographically throughout the world. These trends both contributed to and were furthered by the establishment of powerful "new monarchies" in Western Europe. Lacking such strong, unifying central governments, the splintered states of the Holy Roman Empire, Italy, and much of Eastern Europe fell behind in the international struggle for power. The new statecraft developed in Italy and spread to the rest of Europe.

In "War and Crisis," the international and domestic upheaval between 1560 and 1660, inflamed by religious tensions, will be examined.

ANSWERS

Self Test

1d; 2d; 3a; 4c; 5b; 6d; 7d; 8d; 9d; 10a; 11a; 12b; 13a; 14c; 15c; 16d; 17c; 18c; 19b; 20c; 21b

Guide to Documents

I-1d; I-2a; II-1c

Significant Individuals

1k; 2e; 3n; 4a; 5i; 6d; 7l; 8b; 9p; 10c; 11h; 12o; 13m; 14f; 15g; 16j

Identification

1f; 2d; 3b; 4o; 5m; 6l; 7e; 8j; 9c; 10a; 11g; 12n; 13h; 14p; 15k; 16i

CHRONOLOGICAL DIAGRAM

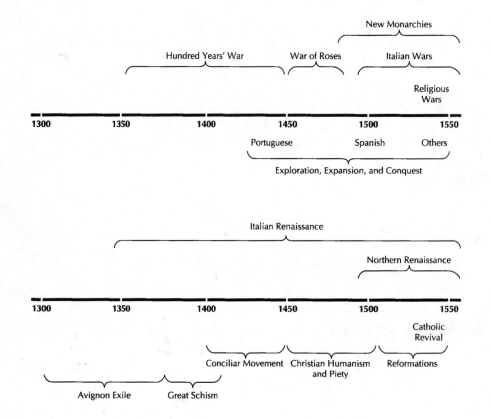

MAP EXERCISES

1.   Indicate the following:

    a. The areas controlled by the various "new monarchies" and the approximate date of the establishment of the "new monarchies."

    b. The areas ruled by Charles V about 1550.

    c. Religious divisions about 1550.

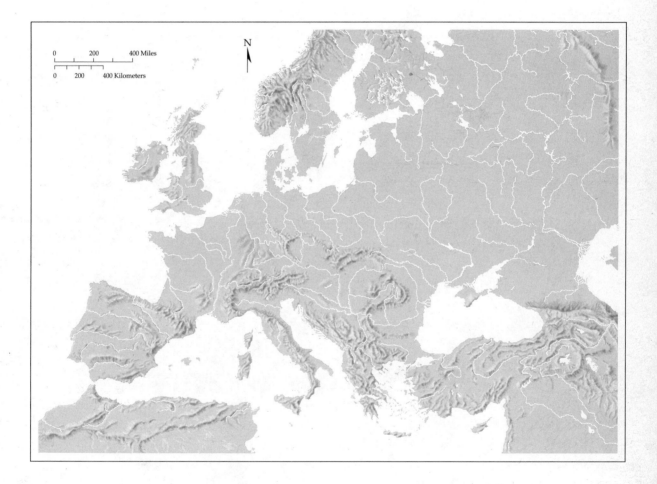

1.   Indicate the areas controlled by the Ottoman Empire about 1560.

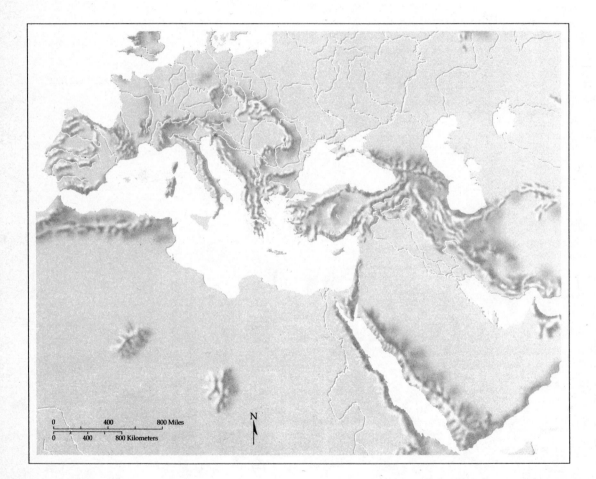

1. Indicate and label those areas of Europe expanding their control to non-Western areas of the world during the fifteenth and sixteenth centuries.

2. Indicate those areas of the non-Western world controlled by European powers by 1560.

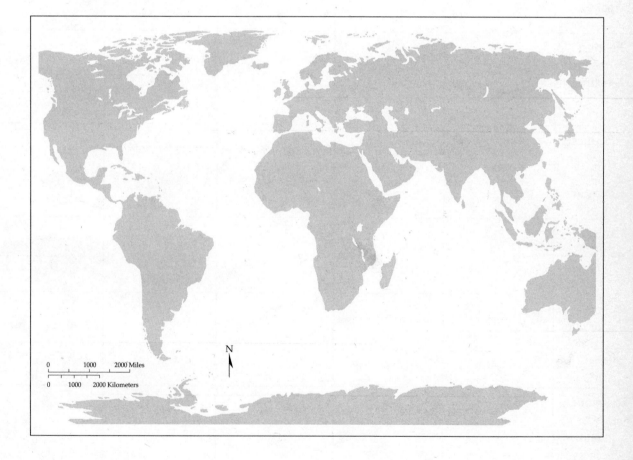

BOX CHART

Reproduce the Box Chart in a larger format in your notebook or on a separate sheet of paper. It is suggested that you devote one page for each column (i.e., chart all seven themes for each country during the period).

For a fuller explanation of the themes and how best to find material, see Introduction.

1300 - 1500

Country Themes	England	France	Spain	Italy	Holy Roman Empire
Social Structure: Groups in Society					
Politics: Events and Structures					
Economics: Production and Distribution					
Family Gender Roles Daily Life					
War: Relationship to larger society					
Religion: Beliefs, Communities, Conflicts					
Cultural Expression: Formal and Popular					

CULTURAL STYLES

1.   Contrast the following three trios of artworks. What similarities are there among the works from the same period? What are the similarities and differences from one period to the next? What are the similarities and differences between the first period and the third?

    a. the paintings on pages 73, 299, and 402

    b. the sculptures on pages 84, 292, and 402

    c. the busts on page 106 and 200 and the painting on page 397;

2.   Contrast the mosaic on page 163 with the painting on page 405 (top). What are the artistic similarities and differences? In what ways do they each embody the age in which they were created?

3.   In what ways does the picture on page 407, both its style and its subject, embody the Renaissance?

4.   Contrast the pictures on pages 408, 405 (bottom), and 406 with those on pages 428, 433, and 430. What do the differences between the two groups suggest about the differences between the Renaissance in Italy and the Renaissance in the North?

5.   What do the painting on page 424 and 457 and the engraving on page 443 suggest about the role of art in the religious controversies of the Reformation.

FIFTEEN
WAR AND CRISIS

CHAPTER HIGHLIGHTS

1. A series of costly, devastating wars, inflamed by religious motives, raged in Europe in the period between the 1560s and 1650s.

2. The most devastating war was the Thirty Years' War. It was brought to an end by the Peace of Westphalia, which signified major international changes and a new period of relative calm.

3. New weapons, tactics, and armies revolutionized war during the period.

4. Throughout Europe tensions created great internal unrest, often breaking out in revolt and civil war.

5. During the mid-seventeenth century, new political patterns were established that would hold for some time.

CHAPTER OUTLINE

I. Rivalry and War in the Age of Philip II

1. Philip II

2. Elizabeth I

3. The Dutch Revolt

4. Civil War in France

II. From Unbounded War to International Crises

1. The Thirty Years' War

2. The Peace of Westphalia

III. The Military Revolution

1. Weapons and Tactics

2. The Organization and Support of Armies

3. The Life of the Soldier

IV. Revolution in England

1. Parliament and the Law

2. Rising Antagonisms

3. Civil War

4. England under Cromwell

V. Revolts in France and Spain

1. The France of Henry IV

2. Louis XIII

3. Political and Social Crisis

4. The Fronde

5. Sources of Discontent in Spain

6. Revolt and Secession

VI. Political Change in an Age of Crisis

1. The United Provinces

2. Sweden

3. Eastern Europe and the "Crisis"

SELF TEST

1. Philip II of Spain dominated the second half of the sixteenth century because of his

    a. insatiable quest for military glory.

    b. determination to defeat the enemies of Catholicism.

    c. goal of securing Spanish dominance of Europe.

    d. desire to restore the empire of his father, Charles V.

2. England's victory over the Spanish Armada accomplished all of the following EXCEPT

    a. preventing an invasion of England by Spanish troops.

    b. enabling England to continue supporting the Dutch rebels.

    c. sparking rebellions in Portugal, Catalonia, Naples, and Sicily.

    d. sealing the fate of Spain's Catholic allies in the French Civil War.

3. The Dutch revolt was all of the following EXCEPT

    a. a national struggle against a foreign overlord.

    b. a religious struggle between Protestants and Catholics.

    c. the first major victory in Europe by subjects resisting their monarch's authority.

    d. the first of the religious wars to end with a treaty ensuring tolerance for both confessions.

4. All of the following were issues in the French Civil War EXCEPT

    a. Philip II's desire to draw France into his dynastic empire.

    b. the struggle between the Protestants and the Catholics.

    c. the rivalry of the Guise and the Bourbon families.

    d. the reassertion of autonomy by the great nobles.

5. All of the following were true of the combatants in the Thirty Years' War EXCEPT

    a. The Habsburgs sought to defeat Protestantism and establish control over the Holy Roman Empire.

    b. The German Catholics sought to advance their religion while avoiding Habsburg domination.

    c. The German Protestants sought to defend their religion and avoid Habsburg domination.

    d. The Swedes, Spanish, and French sought to keep the Empire weak to enhance their own relative strength.

6. The Peace of Westphalia was important for all of the following reasons EXCEPT

    a. it ended the anarchy in Germany.

    b. it secured Spanish control of Holland.

    c. it formalized the fragmentation of Germany.

    d. it laid the groundwork for international relations for the next century.

7. The primary cause of the military revolution was

    a. gunpowder.

    b. pikemen.

    c. sieges.

    d. discipline.

8. Between 1550 and 1700, the size of the leading army in Europe increased

    a. from 40,000 to 60,000 men.

    b. from 40,000 to 100,000 men.

    c. from 40,000 to 200,000 men.

    d. from 40,000 to 400,000 men.

9. The growth of the military caused all of the following to increase EXCEPT

    a. the size of the government bureaucracy needed to support the military.

    b. the amount of taxes needed to support the military.

    c. the amount of damage done by soldiers to the areas they were stationed.

    d. the elaboration of military command and administrative structures.

10. All of the following social groups were centers of opposition to the English monarch EXCEPT

    a. the Puritans.

    b. the gentry.

    c. the nobility.

    d. the merchants.

11. The Petition of Rights called for an end to all of the following EXCEPT

    a. imprisonment without cause shown.

    b. the king's right to dissolve Parliament.

    c. taxation without Parliament's consent.

    d. martial law in peacetime.

12. The major factions in the English Civil War included all of the following EXCEPT

    a.   Royalists, who supported the king once the Grand Remonstrance was passed.

    b.   Presbyterians, Puritans who wanted a centrally organized, Calvinist Church.

    c.   Lutherans, who wanted to make the original Protestantism as the state religion.

    d.   Independents, Puritans who wanted each congregation to rule itself.

13. The English Civil War ended with the Restoration of the Stuart dynasty because

    a.   the people had never supported revolution and turned on the Puritans once Cromwell was dead.

    b.   the rebels were unable to create viable permanent structures.

    c.   Parliament realized that it had acted illegally and wanted to restore the rule of law.

    d.   royalists were able to infiltrate the Parliamentary government and stage a bloodless coup.

14. Henry IV's accomplishments included all of the following EXCEPT

    a.   creating religious peace by converting to Catholicism while guaranteeing the rights of the Protestants.

    b.   reestablishing the authority of the king by buying off the nobility and the principal bureaucrats.

    c.   establishing the notion that the government had primary responsibility to foster economic development.

    d.   leading the French intervention in the Holy Roman Empire that frustrated Habsburg designs.

15. Cardinal Richelieu accomplished all of the following EXCEPT

    a.   reducing the independence of the traditional nobles.

    b.   establishing the *intendents* as dominant officials in the provinces.

    c.   destroying the Huguenots' independent military and political power.

    d.   leading the French to final victory in the Thirty Years' War.

16. The growth of royal power in France caused discontent in all of the following groups EXCEPT

    a.   peasants, who objected to the increasingly onerous taxes.

    b.   officials, who wanted to retain and expand their traditional prerogatives.

    c.   merchants, who opposed the heavy hand of government regulation.

    d.   nobles, who resisted the crowns' reduction of their traditional autonomy.

17. The Fronde failed because of

    a.   Spanish intervention.

    b.   the disunity of the rebels.

    c.   the perfidy of the nobles.

    d.   the prestige of the king.

18. Spain suffered from all of the following problems in the mid-seventeenth century EXCEPT

    a.   the wealth from America had been squandered on wars rather than invested in economic development.

    b.   the bureaucracy was inefficient and dominated by Castilians, who were resented in other provinces.

    c.   devastating plagues reduced the population by 40%, from 10 million to 6 million people.

    d.   foreign enemies had invaded the country and seized its most valuable territories.

19. Which of the following was able to break away from the Spanish control during the revolts at mid-century?

    a.   Portugal.

    b.   Catalonia.

    c.   Sicily.

    d.   Naples.

20. The primary constitutional struggle in the United Provinces was between

    a.   the House of Orange, backed by the rural provinces, and the merchant oligarchy that controlled Holland.

    b.   the House of Orange, backed by the merchant oligarchy in Holland, and the rural provinces.

    c.   the Protestant northern provinces and the Catholic southern ones.

    d.   the Protestant urban provinces and the Catholic rural ones.

21. Gustavus Adolphus accomplished all of the following for Sweden EXCEPT

    a.   he made it the most powerful state in the Baltic area and a major power in Europe.

    b.   he organized a bureaucracy that was superior to most until the twentieth century.

    c.   he tamed the nobility so the country was spared constitutional turmoil for centuries.

    d.   he fostered the development of the country's mines and other economic assets.

22. The Romanov dynasty in Russia accomplished all of the following EXCEPT

    a.   cementing an alliance with the nobility.

    b.   forcing the peasantry into complete subordination.

    c.   codifying the laws and establishing control of the church.

    d.   keeping the Ukraine from switching allegiance to Poland.

GUIDE TO DOCUMENTS

I. Queen Elizabeth's Armada Speech

1. How did Elizabeth attempt to appeal to the troops?

    a.   She emphasized her trust in and commitment to them.

    b.   She played on their chivalric duty to protect her as a woman.

    c.   She emphasized their national superiority over the Spaniards.

    d.   She whipped up their fear and hatred of Catholics.

2. In what ways does she justify her own political power?

II. Oliver Cromwell's Aims

1. Cromwell gives all of the following reasons for declining the offer to serve as king EXCEPT

    a.   he wants Parliament to create the long term basis for peace while he maintains order in the short term.

    b.   he thinks that as Constable he already has sufficient power to settle English peace and liberties.

    c.   God has destroyed the office as well as the person of the king, and he will not go against His Providence.

    d.   the destruction of the monarchy was decided by a prolonged and convulsive process.

2. How does Cromwell's reasoning reflect his religious beliefs and the role religion played in the civil war?

III. Richelieu on Diplomacy

1. All of the following insights conveyed in this excerpt help explain Richelieu's extraordinary success EXCEPT

   a. he pursued every avenue of negotiation that might lead to success, and many did.

   b. he pressed ahead with critical negotiations to maximize the benefit gained from them.

   c. he used his contacts to gain as much information as possible even when the negotiations led nowhere.

   d. he avoided conceding anything of value in negotiations, calculating that eventually he would get his way.

2. In what ways does the document reflect the connections between diplomacy and international interests of the state during this period?

<u>SIGNIFICANT INDIVIDUALS</u>

1.	Philip II	a.	Political philosopher of power and restraint (1530-1596)
2.	Elizabeth I	b.	Mercenary general in Thirty Years' War (1583-1634)
3.	William of Orange	c.	Spanish minister who sparked revolts (r.1621-1643)
4.	Maurice of Nassau	d.	French minister who built up monarchy (r.1624-1642)
5.	Catherine de Medici (MED-a-chē)	e.	Scottish king who became King of England and began struggle with Parliament (r.1603-1625)
6.	Duke of Guise (gēz)	f.	Swedish king and great general (r.1611-1632)
7.	Henry IV	g.	Brilliant military leader of Dutch revolt (1587-1625)
8.	Jean Bodin	h.	French minister who defeated Fronde (r.1642-1661)
9.	Ferdinand II	i.	Independent, general, and ruler of England (1599-1658)
10.	Albrecht von Wallenstein (WOL-en-stīn)	j.	Leader of French Catholics in Wars of Religion (1550-1589)
11.	Gustavus Adolphus (gus-TAH-vus a-DOL-fus)	k.	English queen who defeated Spanish armada (r.1558-1603)
12.	James I	l.	Representative of mercantile Holland (1625-1672)
13.	Charles I	m.	French king during Thirty Years War (r.1610-1643)
14.	Oliver Cromwell	n.	Initial leader of Dutch revolt (1533-1584)
15.	Louis XIII	o.	English king who lost his head (r.1625-1649)
16.	Cardinal Richelieu (rē-shuh-LYOO)	p.	Regent during French Wars of Religion (1519-1589)
17.	Cardinal Mazarin (MAZ-e-rin)	q.	Emperor who provoked Thirty Years War (r.1619-1637)
18.	Count of Olivares (Ŏ-lē-var-ez)	r.	French king who ended Wars of Religion (r.1589-1610)
19.	Jan De Witt (yahn de wit)	s.	King of Spain at its height of power (r.1556-1598)

CHRONOLOGICAL DIAGRAM

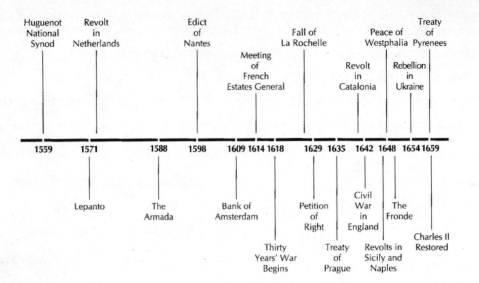

IDENTIFICATION

1. Spanish Armada

2. Huguenots (HYOO-ge-nots)

3. the Catholic League

4. *politiques* (pol-i-TIKS)

5. Edict of Nantes (nahnts)

6. Peace of Westphalia (west-FĂ-lē-a)

7. the salvo

8. Grand Remonstrance

9. "Long" Parliament

10. New Model Army

11. "Rump" Parliament

12. Levellers

13. *paulette* (pol-et)

14. mercantilism

15. *intendant* (in-TEN-dant)

16. the Fronde (frond)

17. Union of Arms

a. Treaty that framed European diplomatic order after 1648

b. Fleet that tried to invade England

c. Series of revolts in mid-seventeenth century France

d. Tactic of having all musketeers fire at once

e. Representative body that sat through English Civil War

f. Force commanded by Cromwell

g. French faction in favor of stability through monarchy

h. Doctrine that government should build up economy

i. Military organization of French Catholics

j. English social revolutionaries

k. French royal official used to reduce local nobles' power

l. French royal decree setting limited religious toleration

m. Sum of legislation passed at begging of English Civil War

n. French Protestants

o. Plan to unify Spanish administration

p. Representative body minus royalists and Presbyterians

q. Fee making purchased offices hereditary

174

MAP EXERCISES

1.   Indicate those areas under the rule of Philip II of Spain. What does this reveal about some of the problems facing him?

2.   Indicate areas of Protestant resistance to the religious policies of Philip II.

1. Indicate the lands controlled by the Austrian Habsburgs, the Spanish Habsburgs, France, Brandenburg-Prussia, and Sweden in 1660.

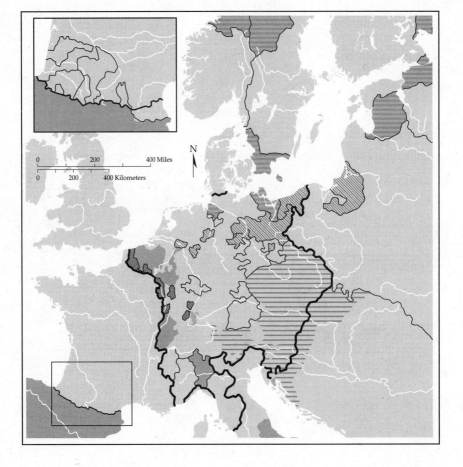

PROBLEMS FOR ANALYSIS

I. Rivalry and War in the Age of Philip II

1. Evaluate the relative weight of religious and political factors underlying the wars between the 1560s and 1640s.

2. What problems faced Philip II?

II. From Unbounded War to International Crises

1. In what ways does the Thirty Years' War reflect the mixture of politics and religion in war during this period?

2. What was the significance of the Peace of Westphalia?

III. The Military Revolution

1. What changes in military equipment, tactics, and organization took place during the sixteenth and seventeenth centuries? What were some of the economic, social, and political consequences of these changes?

IV. Revolution in England

1. How do you explain the civil war and revolution in England? Were opponents clearly split along religious or social lines?

2. What role did Cromwell play during this period?

V. Revolts in France and Spain

1. Compare the issues that caused discord in France and England. Is it fair to consider the Fronde similar to the English revolution? Why?

2. How do you explain Spain's decline in the seventeenth century? Evaluate the role economic factors played in this decline.

VI. Political Change in an Age of Crisis

1. What was so unusual about the United Provinces? How would you explain its rapid economic and cultural success?

2. How was Sweden able to rise from a second-rate power to a position of dominance in the Baltic during the seventeenth century? What policies did Gustavus Adolphus follow to this end?

3. Compare the general nature of constitutional settlements reached throughout Europe at mid-century. In what areas did monarchical power prevail? In what areas was monarchical power weakened?

SPECULATIONS

1. How might Charles I have prevented the English Civil War and revolution?

2. As a political leader in the early seventeenth century, would you use religion for your own ends? What are the dangers in doing or not doing this?

3. As adviser to Philip II of Spain, what policies would you recommend to prevent the eventual decline of Spanish power? Why?

TRANSITIONS

In "Economic Expansion and a New Politics," the economic advances during the late-fifteenth century and the sixteenth century, the process of European expansion, and the growth of political authority around the "new monarchs" of Western Europe were examined.

In "War and Crisis," we see the period between the 1560s and 1650s dominated by war and internal revolt. Politics and religion entwined in these upheavals, above all in the civil wars in England and France and the Thirty Years' War in the Holy Roman Empire. The period ends with a relative sense of constitutional and military stability in most places, which was to last for some time.

In "Culture and Society in the Age of the Scientific Revolution," the social, cultural, and intellectual patterns paralleling these political and international trends during the sixteenth and seventeenth centuries will be explored.

ANSWERS

Self Test

1b; 2c; 3d; 4a; 5d; 6b; 7a; 8d; 9c; 10c; 11b; 12c; 13b; 14d; 15d; 16c; 17b; 18d; 19a; 20a; 21c; 22d

Guide to Documents

I-1a; II-1b; III-1d

Significant Individuals

1s; 2k; 3n; 4g; 5p; 6j; 7r; 8a; 9q; 10b; 11f; 12e; 13o; 14i; 15m; 16d; 17h; 18c; 19l

Identification

1b; 2n; 3i; 4g; 5l; 6a; 7d; 8m; 9e; 10f; 11p; 12j; 13q; 14h; 15k; 16c; 17o

SIXTEEN
CULTURE AND SOCIETY IN THE AGE OF THE SCIENTIFIC REVOLUTION

MAIN THEMES

1. Major breakthroughs in physics, astronomy, mathematics, and anatomy resting on the new scientific principles of reason, doubt, observation, generalization, and testing by experiment overturned accepted ideas about nature and laid the foundations for modern science.

2. Cultural styles evolved, from the distortion of Mannerism to the drama of the Baroque and the discipline of Classicism.

3. Seventeenth-century society was hierarchical, although mobility was becoming increasingly common in the higher orders.

4. The traditional village was changing and being pulled into the activities of the territorial state, a process that often involved wrenching dislocations for the people involved.

5. While general attitudes were marked by belief in magic and mystical forces, these came to have less impact on public policy and the general culture as educated opinion became increasingly skeptical of them.

6. Both elite and popular culture generally followed a trajectory from passion and turmoil to restraint and order similar to the transition in politics and international relations during the same period.

OUTLINE AND SUMMARY

I. The Scientific Revolution

1. Origins of the Scientific Revolution

2. The Breakthroughs

3. Kepler and Galileo

4. Isaac Newton

II. The Effects of the Discoveries

1. A New Epistemology

2. The Wider Influence of Scientific Thought

3. Bacon and Descartes

4. Blaise Pascal

5. Science Institutionalized

III. Literature and the Arts

1. Mannerism

2. Michel de Montaigne

3. Cervantes and Shakespeare

4. The Baroque: Grandeur and Excitement

5. Classicism: Grandeur and Restraint

IV. Social Patterns and Popular Culture

1. Population Trends

2. Social Status

3. Mobility and Crime

4. Change in the Village

5. City Life

6. Popular Culture in the City

7. Magic and Rituals

8. Witchcraft

9. Forces of Restraint

SELF TEST

1. All of the following helped set the scientific revolution in motion EXCEPT

    a. inaccuracies in and inconsistencies among ancient authorities.

    b. magical beliefs that emphasized simple, comprehensive keys to nature.

    c. belief in the importance of observation and development of instruments.

    d. changes in Christianity that focused on its metaphorical rather than literal truth.

2. Which of the following was NOT one of the important scientific breakthroughs in the sixteenth century?

    a. Vesalius' anatomical studies.

    b. Copernicus' astronomy.

    c. Kepler's laws of planetary motion.

    d. Tycho Brahe's observations of the heavens.

3. Which of the following were NOT critical developments in astronomy and physics?

    a. Galileo's concept of inertia and his observations of the moons of Jupiter.

    b. Kepler's laws of planetary motion and his synthesis of them with terrestrial physics.

    c. Descartes development of analytic geometry and distinction between weight and mass.

    d. Newton's development of calculus and his three laws of motion.

4. Newton's work was the culmination of the scientific revolution because

    a. it resolved the outstanding problems in both physics and astronomy.

    b. it refuted Descartes' theoretical approach to scientific knowledge.

    c. it reconciled science with Christianity as it was then understood.

    d. it made further work unnecessary for the next 150 years.

5. The new epistemology of science involved all of the following EXCEPT

 a. reliance on experience and reason rather than authority.

 b. testing of an hypothesis by observation, generalization, and experimentation.

 c. rejection of Occam's theory that the simplest explanation is best.

 d. use of numerical data to develop mathematical laws.

6. Wider acceptance of scientific thought came when the educated public

 a. became convinced that science offered certainty.

 b. accepted that science cannot promise certainty.

 c. made the effort to follow the intricacies of scientific debate.

 d. became enamored of the charismatic figures of science.

7. Bacon and Descartes complemented each other because

 a. they had long been ardent admirers of each other.

 b. Bacon emphasized experiment and inductive reasoning while Descartes emphasized deductive analysis.

 c. Bacon was able to influence his fellow Englishmen, while Descartes worked on the French.

 d. they both were able to refute Newton's work by approaching it from opposite points of view.

8. Blaise Pascal is important because

 a. he promoted a reconciliation of Catholic faith with the new science.

 b. he kept European civilization from accepting the mechanical world view.

 c. he was the first accomplished scientist to focus on the limitations of science.

 d. he was able to undercut some of the extreme claims of science on a scientific basis.

9. All of the following were examples of popular enthusiasm for science in the late seventeenth century EXCEPT

 a. royal patronage of scientific societies.

 b. the use of science as an aristocratic amusement.

 c. popular attendance at autopsies.

 d. the widespread practice of *charivaris*.

10. The primary impulse behind Mannerism was

 a. distortion.

 b. escapism.

 c. mysticism.

 d. singularity.

11. Michel de Montagne created the literary form known as the

 a. essay.

 b. novel.

 c. reflections.

 d. epigram.

12. Cervantes and Shakespeare had in common that they both

    a. were Englishmen.

    b. had essentially optimistic outlooks.

    c. reflected the stresses of their times.

    d. rejected the hierarchy of society.

13. The Baroque style was found particularly in Catholic countries because

    a. it supported the Counter Reformation.

    b. only they had the wealth to support it.

    c. Protestants preferred more flamboyant styles.

    d. only there were artists with necessary skills found.

14. The Classical style was differentiated from the Baroque because

    a. it was characterized by restraint and discipline.

    b. it aimed at grandiose effects.

    c. it was found mainly in Protestant countries.

    d. it included art forms beyond painting.

15. The number of Europeans rose only slightly in the seventeenth century for all the following reasons EXCEPT

    a. economic pressures caused people to marry late, which reduced the number of babies they could have.

    b. the Thirty Years' War killed millions of Germans and disrupted the European economy.

    c. plagues drove the number of Spaniards down from 10 million in 1600 to 6 million in 1700.

    d. the English and Dutch populations only recovered after 1680, accounting for the little increase there was.

16. Seventeenth century society was characterized by

    a. impenetrable class barriers.

    b. relative egalitarianism.

    c. significant mobility.

    d. decreasing stratification.

17. Life was generally becoming harder for the peasantry for all of the following reasons EXCEPT

    a. taxes were rising.

    b. rents and other dues were increasing.

    c. food prices were stabilizing.

    d. there was no escape from the farm.

18. All of the following changes were taking place in traditional villages EXCEPT

    a. differences in wealth among the peasants were increasing.

    b. government officials were eroding village self-government.

    c. government welfare programs were enticing peasants off the land.

    d. noble landlords were ceasing to pay attention to their villagers' lives.

19. In contrast to the villages, life in the cities was

    a.   secure.

    b.   impersonal.

    c.   dull.

    d.   fragile.

20. All of the following first became common in cities in the late seventeenth century EXCEPT

    a.   weekly newspapers.

    b.   coffeehouses.

    c.   actresses.

    d.   books.

21. Urban and rural culture were distinguished by all of the following EXCEPT

    a.   literacy rates.

    b.   magical beliefs.

    c.   types of recreation.

    d.   visibility of religiosity.

22. The witch craze was caused by all of the following EXCEPT

    a.   an intention to persecute innocent people.

    b.   popular fears that bad effects can be willed.

    c.   an official desires to root out agents of evil.

    d.   a fear of women who seemed too potent.

23. The decline of witch-hunting occurred for all of the following reasons EXCEPT

    a.   official recognition that it was disruptive and dangerous.

    b.   the rising cultural weight of cities, where events are more subject to rational human control.

    c.   religious changes that de-emphasized magic and disapproved of passionate popular activities.

    d.   the rapid spread of the scientific world view to all classes of society.

GUIDE TO DOCUMENTS

I. Galileo and Kepler on Copernicus

1. Aside from their personalities, what seems in these passages to explain why Kepler is more open than Galileo?

    a.   He is more convinced Copernicus is right.

    b.   His is the more powerful mind.

    c.   He lives in a more tolerant country.

    d.   He thinks fewer scholars still oppose Copernicus.

2. What does this reveal about the potential strength of the new scientific community in Europe?

II. A Witness Analyzes the Witch Craze

1. According to Linden, what was the primary dynamic driving the witch-hunts?

   a. Witches caused bad harvests; so the people and government prosecuted them.

   b. The irrational fears of the populace drove them to carry out mob justice.

   c. Corrupt officials created a scandal about witches in order to make a profit.

   d. Corrupt officials exploited popular fears in order to make a profit.

2. What were some of the forces that led to the decline of the witch-hunts?

IDENTIFICATION

1. alchemy (AL-ke-mē)   a. Core principals of Newton's physics

2. scientific method   b. Catholic mystical movement stressing faith

3. three laws of motion   c. First scientific journal

4. mechanism   d. Movement by landlords to squeeze more out of peasants

5. Skepticism   e. Campaign to eradicate evil magicians

6. Jansenism   f. Short name of Newton's primary work

7. Royal Society of London   g. Philosophy of doubt

8. *Philosophical Transactions*   h. Cultural style emphasizing grandeur and excitement

9. *Principia*   i. Rituals believed to transform one substance into another

10. Baroque (ba-RŎK)   j. Theory that universe is a machine subject to physical laws

11. seigniorial reaction   k. Process of hypothesis, observation, generalization, and
    (sēn-YOR-ē-al)   experimentation

12. witch craze   l. Group that promoted scientific research

CHRONOLOGICAL DIAGRAM

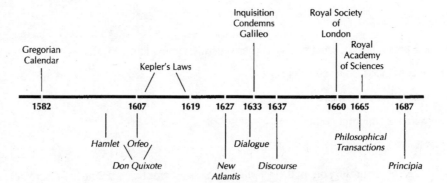

SIGNIFICANT INDIVIDUALS

1. Andreas Vesalius (vi-SĀ-lē-us)

2. Nicolaus Copernicus (kō-PUR-ni-Kus)

3. William Harvey

4. Johannes Kepler (KEP-luhr)

5. Galileo Galilei (gal-uh-LĒ-ō gal-uh-LĀ)

6. Isaac Newton

7. Francis Bacon

8. René Descartes (dā-KART)

9. Blaise Pascal (pas-KAL)

10. El Greco (GREK-ō)

11. Michel de Montaigne (mon-TĀN)

12. Miguel de Cervantes (ser-VAN-tēz)

13. William Shakespeare

14. Caravaggio (ka-ra-VAD-jō)

15. Peter Paul Rubens

16. GianLorenzo Bernini (JĒ-an LO-ren-zō ber-NĒ-nē)

17. Rembrandt van Rijn (ryn)

18. Caludio Monteverdi (mon-tā-VER-dē)

19. Nicholas Poussin (poo-san)

20. Pierre Corneille (kor-NĀ)

21. Jean Racine (ra-SĒN)

a. Scientist who formulated the laws of motion (1642-1727)

b. Astronomer who determined that the planets' orbits are elliptical (1571-1630)

c. Philosopher who emphasized deduction (1596-1650)

d. French Classical painter (1594-1665)

e. Originator of Baroque style (1571-1610)

f. Premier English playwright (1564-1616)

g. Baroque sculptor and architect (1598-1680)

h. Philosopher who emphasized induction (1561-1626)

i. Dutch painter who transcended style (1606-1669)

j. Leading Flemish Baroque painter (1577-1640)

k. Anatomist who discovered that the heart pumps blood (1578-1626)

l. French playwright uneasy with Classicism who wrote *Le Cid* (1606-1684)

m. Creator of opera and orchestra (1567-1643)

n. Leading skeptic and essayist (1533-1592)

o. Model French Classical playwright (1639-1699)

p. Astronomer who said the Earth circles the Sun (1473-1543)

q. Author of *Don Quixote* (1547-1616)

r. Scientist who created the concept of inertia, built a telescope, and discovered Jupiter's moons (1564-1643)

s. Anatomist who found Galen inaccurate (1514-1564)

t. Scientist who questioned science (1623-1662)

u. Leading Mannerist painter (1548?-1625?)

MAP EXERCISE

1. Label the five cities that grew most rapidly between 1500 and 1800.
2. Indicate and label Europe's eight largest cities in 1700.

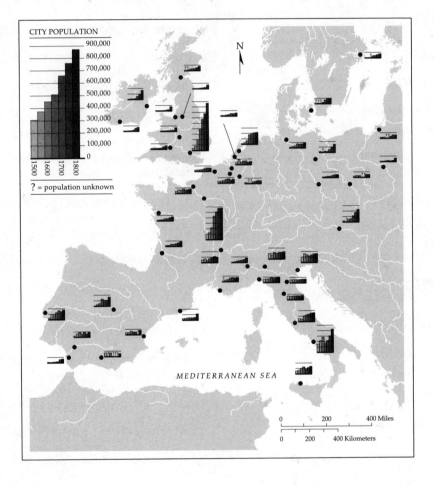

PROBLEMS FOR ANALYSIS

I. The Scientific Revolution

1. Explain the origins of the scientific revolution. Were the theories of the ancient Greeks a hindrance or a support? What role did magical beliefs play?

2. What was the essence of the conflict between Galileo and the Church? Do you think it was in the Church's interest to condemn Galileo? Why?

II. The Effects of the Discoveries

1. Use examples to demonstrate the principles of the scientific method. How does the scientific method differ from earlier methods of obtaining and verifying knowledge?

2. Compare the methods emphasized by Francis Bacon, René Descartes, and Isaac Newton. Do you think that Blaise Pascal would disagree with the methods and concerns of these men? Why?

III. Literature and the Arts

1. Compare the Baroque and Classical styles. In what ways did they reflect other developments in sixteenth- and seventeenth-century Europe?

2. It has been argued that Cervantes and Shakespeare reflected the historical concerns of their own societies as well as timeless human concerns. Use examples to support this argument.

IV. Social Patterns and Popular Culture

1. How was seventeenth-century society organized? Compare the possibilities for social mobility among various social groups.

2. What were some of the demographic characteristics of seventeenth-century society? How do you explain population patterns in the seventeenth century?

3. How did popular culture reflect a dependence on nature and the conditions of life among the peasantry? How does the great witch craze fit into this situation?

4. What were the causes for change in the traditional village? Were most of these causes internal, or were they a result of intrusions from the outside?

SPECULATIONS

1. The scientific revolution profoundly changed the ways in which people thought. It was difficult for many to accept this change. Today scientific ways of thinking are as accepted and taken for granted as traditional ways of thinking in the sixteenth century. What might a future change in the ways of thinking be like, and do you think such ways of thinking would be accepted without too much difficulty?

2. Imagine what a debate between Galileo and the head of the Inquisition would be like? Write a script for this exchange as if you were writing a play, including both their words and their expressions and gestures.

3. Are there any parallels between the great witch craze of the seventeenth century and more recent historical occurrences? Explain.

TRANSITIONS

In "War and Crisis," a period of violence and upheaval marked by unusually brutal warfare was examined. It was not until the mid-seventeenth century that the violence subsided and a new sense of order was attained.

In "Culture and Society in the Age of the Scientific Revolution," cultural and social patterns are shown to reflect this progression from uncertainty to stable resolution. This is clearest in the triumph of the scientific revolution—the revolutionary discoveries of a handful of men who laid the foundations for modern science—but it is also apparent in the evolution from Mannerism to the Classical style and in the increased control over people's lives gained by central governments. The upper classes throughout Europe benefited most from these trends.

In "The Emergence of the European State System," the course of political history during the second half of the seventeenth century will be explored. In this period absolutist kings continue the process of state building within a European society dominated by the aristocracy.

ANSWERS

Self Test

1d; 2c; 3b; 4a; 5c; 6a; 7b; 8c; 9d; 10b; 11a; 12c; 13a; 14a; 15d; 16c; 17d; 18c; 19b; 20d; 21b; 22a; 23d

Guide to Documents

I-1c; II-1d

Significant Individuals

1s; 2p; 3k; 4b; 5r; 6a; 7h; 8c; 9t; 10u; 11n; 12q; 13f; 14e; 15j; 16g; 17i; 18m; 19d; 20l; 21o

Identification

1i; 2k; 3a; 4j; 5g; 6b; 7l; 8c; 9f; 10h; 11d; 12e

SEVENTEEN

THE EMERGENCE OF THE EUROPEAN STATE SYSTEM

CHAPTER HIGHLIGHTS

1. Louis XIV—by making his court at Versailles the center of society and by building the state's power through financial, domestic, and military policies—epitomized the absolutist monarchs of the late seventeenth century.

2. In related ways, absolutism grew in Austria, Prussia, Russia, and, to a lesser extent, Spain.

3. The governments of England, the United Provinces, Sweden, and Poland were dominated by aristocrats or merchants. With the exception of England, these countries suffered a decline in power and influence.

4. During the eighteenth century the states of Europe competed for authority and prestige within a system that created a balance of power.

CHAPTER OUTLINE

I. The Creation of Absolutism in France

1. Louis XIV at Versailles

2. Government

3. Foreign Policy

4. Domestic Policy

5. The Condition of France

6. France after Louis XIV

II. Austrian and Prussian Absolutism

1. The Habsburgs at Vienna

2. The Hohenzollerns at Berlin

3. Rivalry and State Building

4. The Prussia of Frederick William I

5. Frederick the Great

6. The Habsburg Empire

7. Maria Theresa

III. Absolutism in Spain and Russia

1. The Habsburgs and Bourbons at Madrid

2. Peter the Great at St. Petersburg

IV. Alternatives to Absolutism

1. Aristocracy in the United Provinces, Sweden, and Poland

2. The Triumph of the Gentry in England

3. Politics and Prosperity

4. The Growth of Stability

5. Contrasts in Political Thought

V. The International System

1. Diplomacy and Warfare

2. Armies and Navies

3. The Seven Years' War

SELF TEST

1. Louis XIV's court at Versailles was designed to serve all of the following purposes EXCEPT

   a. to impress people with his wealth, power, and refinement.

   b. to insulate the court from the turmoil of the capital city.

   c. to serve as a final defensive bastion in case of invasion.

   d. to detach nobles from their traditional bases of power in the provinces.

2. Developing the country's bureaucracy gave Louis increased ability to do all of the following EXCEPT

   a. expand and control the armed forces.

   b. formulate and execute laws.

   c. collect and disburse revenue.

   d. disenfranchise the traditional nobility.

3. Louis' foreign policy resulted in

   a. decisive victories.

   b. greater gains than losses.

   c. only marginal gains at great cost.

   d. great losses of territory and resources.

4. Louis XIV's domestic policy included all of the following EXCEPT

   a. fostering manufacturing, agriculture, and trade.

   b. expelling the Huguenots and suppressing Jansenism.

   c. quashing legal protests and crushing peasant rebellions.

   d. transforming the aristocracy into a compulsory service class.

5. From late in Louis XIV's reign through the middle of Louis XV's, conditions in France generally went

    a.   from bad to worse.

    b.   from good to bad.

    c.   from bad to better.

    d.   from good to better.

6. After Louis XIV, the French monarchy was troubled by all of the following EXCEPT

    a.   renewed competition from aristocrats (especially in the parlements).

    b.   financial instability (thanks to exemptions from taxes enjoyed by the privileged).

    c.   incessant warfare (thanks to Louis XV's dynastic ambitions in Spain).

    d.   political weakness (except during the ministry of Cardinal Fleury).

7. Leopold I of Austria's rule was characterized by all of the following EXCEPT

    a.   establishment of a Versailles-like palace at Schönbrunn.

    b.   reliance on aristocrats to help rule nationally and locally.

    c.   strong efforts to make Imperial rule effective in Germany.

    d.   significant expansion to the southeast at Ottoman expense.

8. Frederick William made Brandenburg-Prussia into a power in Germany by all of the following EXCEPT

    a.   building a strong army, which rose from 8,000 men in 1648 to 22,000 in the 1650s (and 200,000 in 1786).

    b.   allying with the nobles, who got control of the peasants and through serfdom made their estates profitable.

    c.   organizing the state to sustain the army by having officers run the treasury and local administration.

    d.   gaining the title of King in Prussia and making Berlin into a cosmopolitan social and cultural center.

9. International competition spurred internal state building because

    a.   an efficient bureaucracy, prosperous economy, and stable society were the foundations of military power.

    b.   as conquered peoples came under different rulers, they made use of the best aspects of each government.

    c.   larger powers were able to swallow up smaller states wholesale, and had to digest and integrate them.

    d.   rulers vied for the distinction of ruling the most fortunate state by best serving the needs of their people.

10. Frederick William I did all of the following EXCEPT

    a.   increase the size of the army.

    b.   improve the quality of the officers.

    c.   wear an army uniform at all times.

    d.   fight a war.

11. Frederick the Great was all of the following EXCEPT

    a.   an outstanding general.

    b.   a God-fearing German Protestant.

    c.   a composer, poet, and philosopher.

    d.   a ruthless statesman.

12. The Habsburgs faced all of the following difficulties in forging their empire EXCEPT

    a.   it was made up of socially and culturally diverse territories united only by the dynasty that ruled them.

    b.   the local nobles in the different territories jealously defended, and tried to extend, their traditional rights.

    c.   Prussia, France, Spain, and Bavaria tried to take advantage of the succession of Maria Theresa, a woman.

    d.   they lost a number of provinces because Hungarian troops and British gold proved insufficient support.

13. Maria Theresa accomplished all of the following EXCEPT

    a.   expanding Austria's tax base.

    b.   founding new monasteries.

    c.   reforming the administration.

    d.   modernizing the army.

14. Spain remained an important international player in the eighteenth century because of its

    a.   large population.

    b.   powerful navy.

    c.   victorious army.

    d.   economic strength.

15. Peter the Great accomplished all of the following during his reign EXCEPT

    a.   establishing Russia as a major presence in the Black Sea.

    b.   beginning the westernization of Russia's economy and society.

    c.   taking control of the Church and ignoring representative institutions.

    d.   reducing the peasants to the level of serfs and forcing the nobles to serve the state.

16. Holland, Sweden, and Poland in the eighteenth century had in common that

    a.   they lost out because they failed to modernize their political systems.

    b.   they lost out to neighbors who mobilized superior national power.

    c.   they lost out because they overextended themselves when successful.

    d.   they lost out when they could not successfully defend their territory.

17. The Glorious Revolution confirmed the gentry's control of England in all of the following ways EXCEPT

    a.   it reconfirmed that the monarchy did not have the power to defy Parliament.

    b.   it established that the king's ministers were also responsible to Parliament.

    c.   William III accepted legal restraints on his power in exchange for the crown.

    d.   James II took refuge with Louis XIV, identifying absolutism with the enemy.

18. All of the following both contributed to and resulted from England's economic prosperity EXCEPT

    a.   the success of the Bank of England.

    b.   the rise of the Navy.

    c.   Tory dominance in politics.

    d.   overseas expansion.

19. All of the following changes took place in eighteenth century Britain EXCEPT

    a.   The House of Commons came to be dominated by landowners and leading townsmen.

    b.   Britain created a bureaucratized state with a standing army and expanding navy.

    c.   Executive power came to be directed by a cabinet of ministers responsible to Parliament.

    d.   Dominance in setting foreign policy shifted from the landholders to the commercial elite.

20. The main difference between Hobbes and Locke was that Locke argued

    a.   people in nature have liberty but not security.

    b.   government is created by a contract to secure people's lives and property.

    c.   the sovereign is a party to the contract, and may be overthrown if he breaks it.

    d.   if the sovereign is overthrown, people revert to a state of nature.

21. During the eighteenth century, international relations came to be dominated by all of the following EXCEPT

    a.   the impersonal interests of the states rather than the dynastic concerns of the rulers.

    b.   an aristocratic, cosmopolitan, French-speaking corps of professional diplomats.

    c.   the belief that any means were justified in the pursuit of power.

    d.   a balance of power that protected every state's security.

22. During the eighteenth century, all of the following were true of armies and navies EXCEPT

    a.   they became much larger and more expensive.

    b.   officers and men became more professional.

    c.   fighting was restrained by the costs of equipment and trained manpower.

    d.   weapons and tactics changed radically as new technologies were developed.

23. The Seven Years' War was fought by

    a.   England and Prussia against Austria, France, and Russia.

    b.   England and Russia against Austria, France, and Prussia.

    c.   France and Austria against England, Prussia, and Russia.

    d.   France and Russia against England, Austria, and Prussia.

GUIDE TO DOCUMENTS

I. Louis XIV on Kingship

1. What, for Louis XIV, is the ultimate source of monarchical authority?

    a.   A covenant with the people.

    b.   Divine right.

    c.   The realities of power.

    d.   The king's virtue.

2. According to Louis XIV, in what ways should the monarch act?

II. Locke on the Origins of Government

1. According to Locke, why do men exit the state of nature and form a society with a government?

   a. To maintain their liberty.

   b. To take control of others.

   c. To safeguard their property.

   d. To achieve the common good.

2. What, according to Locke, are the limits of society's power over the individual?

III. Maria Theresa in Vehement Mood

1. How does Maria Theresa justify her diplomatic realignment?

   a. She saw her opportunity and took it.

   b. The good of the Austrian people.

   c. England betrayed her first.

   d. Alliance with Russia was more important than with England.

2. What, according to Maria Theresa, are Austria's proper reasons of state?

IDENTIFICATION

1.	Versailles (ver-SĪ)	a.	Prussian nobles
2.	Grand Alliance	b.	Diplomatic agreement recognizing Maria Theresa
3.	Peace of Utrecht (YOO-trekt)	c.	English party for royal power and against war
4.	Act of Toleration	d.	Needs of the government that override other concerns
5.	*vingtième* (van-tã-em)	e.	Leopold I's palace
6.	Junkers (YOONG-kers)	f.	Treaty that ended the War of Spanish Succession
7.	the War Chest	g.	English party against royal power and for war
8.	Schönbrun (SCHOEN-brun)	h.	Theory that a newborn baby's brain is a blank slate
9.	Pragmatic Sanction	i.	Law establishing religious freedom in England
10.	Bill of Rights	j.	Louis XIV's palace
11.	Whigs (hwigs)	k.	New set of alliances and enmities
12.	Tories	l.	Louis XIV's opponents in War of Spanish Succession
13.	*tabula rasa* (TAB-yoo-la RA-sa)	m.	Law on succession, Parliament's powers, and civil rights
14.	reasons of state	n.	French tax intended to tap the wealth of all classes
15.	the diplomatic revolution	o.	Prussian treasury department

CHRONOLOGICAL DIAGRAM

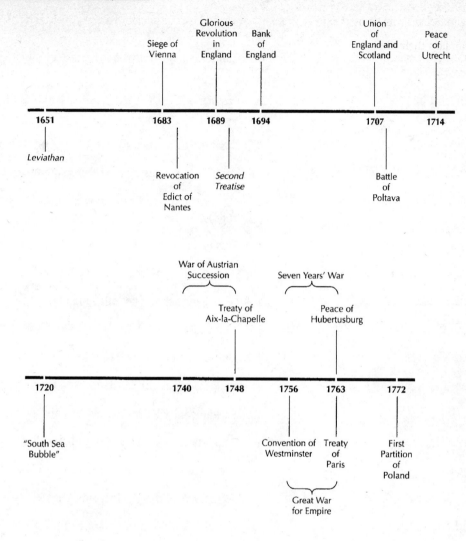

SIGNIFICANT INDIVIDUALS

1. Louis XIV
2. Jean-Baptiste Colbert (kol-BAIR)
3. Marquis de Louvois (lou-VWAH)
4. Louis XV
5. Cardinal Fleury (flue-RĔ)
6. Frederick William, the Great Elector
7. Frederick William I
8. Frederick the Great
9. Maria Theresa
10. Peter the Great
11. Charles XII
12. Charles II
13. James II
14. William III
15. George I
16. Robert Walpole
17. William Pitt
18. Thomas Hobbes (hobz)
19. John Locke (lok)

a. King of France known as the Sun King (r.1643-1715)
b. Empress of Austria who lost Silesia (r. 1740-1780)
c. Prussian king who built up army but didn't fight (r.1701-1740)
d. Louis XIV's advisor to who focused on war (1641-1691)
e. Louis XIV's advisor who focused on money (1619-1683)
f. Leader who made Brandenburg-Prussia a power (r.1640-1688)
g. Pessimistic political philosopher (1588-1679)
h. Restored king of England (1660-1685)
i. "First" prime minister of England (r.1721-1742)
j. Chief advisor to Louis XV (r.1720-1740)
k. Dutch king of England (r.1689-1702)
l. Philosopher of "Life, Liberty, and Property" (1632-1704)
m. Parliamentary leader in Seven Years' War (r.1708-1778)
n. Tsar who modernized Russia (1682-1725)
o. First Hanoverian king of England (r.1714-1727)
p. Aggressive and lucky Prussian king (r.1740-1786)
q. Swedish king who lost empire (1697-1718)
r. French monarch in eighteenth century (1715-1774)
s. English king until Glorious Revolution (1685-1688)

MAP EXERCISE

1. Label the main countries and empires in Europe in 1715.

2. Indicate areas where Louis XIV made efforts to expand France.

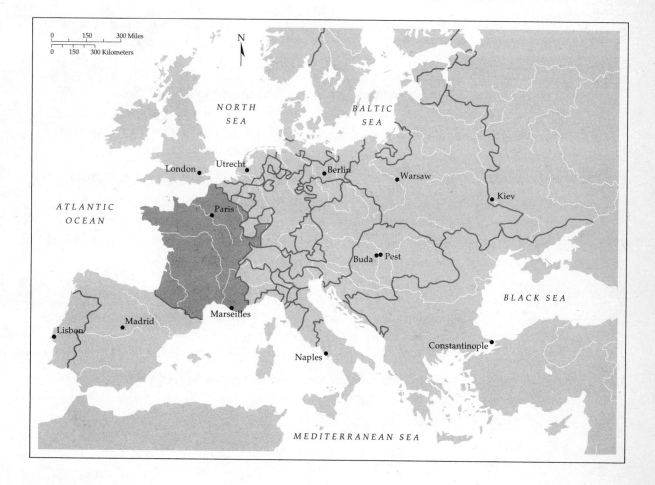

PROBLEMS FOR ANALYSIS

I. The Creation of Absolutism in France

1. In what ways did the policies of Louis XIV build the state's power? What evidences success or failure of these policies?

2. Which of the two views of Louis XIV's reign on page 588 do you find more persuasive? Why?

II. Austrian and Prussian Absolutism

1. Explain the relative success of Prussia during the eighteenth century.

2. How did Austria centralize state power during this period?

III. Absolutism in Spain and Russia

1. Compare Russian absolutism to that of France and Prussia. In what ways was it similar to each? How was it different from both?

IV. Alternatives to Absolutism

1. What developments support the argument that during the late seventeenth century the gentry triumphed in England?

2. Compare the decentralization of government and society that occurred in the United Provinces, Sweden, and Poland during the late seventeenth and early eighteenth centuries.

V. The International System

1. Compare the nature of war and diplomacy during the eighteenth century with that of the late sixteenth and early seventeenth centuries.

2. What role did "reasons of state" and dynastic interests play in the wars, diplomacy, and internal policies of European states during the eighteenth century? Give examples.

SPECULATIONS

1. First as an aristocrat, and second as a merchant, what were the advantages and disadvantages of living in a country dominated by an absolutist monarch?

2. How did Hobbes and Locke disagree with each other?

3. How might Machiavelli view political, diplomatic, and military developments during the eighteenth century? How might Hobbes?

TRANSITIONS

In "Culture and Society in the Age of the Scientific Revolution," the fundamental scientific discoveries and the cultural creations of this period were examined. These achievements contributed to a sense of order by the mid-seventeenth century.

In "The Emergence of the European State System," the quest for order remained the underlying concern throughout Europe. Absolutist kings, epitomized by Louis XIV, rose to prominence. With the exception of England, those states that failed to focus power on the monarch declined. The aristocracy, to varying degrees, dominated the new, powerful governmental administration as needed allies and agents of absolute monarchs or as direct controllers of events. During the eighteenth century international competition was reflected in efforts to further build the state internally.

In "The Wealth of Nations," the new social and economic developments as well as the development of eighteenth-century empires will be examined.

ANSWERS

Self Test

1c; 2d; 3c; 4d; 5c; 6c; 7c; 8d; 9a; 10d; 11b; 12d; 13b; 14b; 15a; 16b; 17b; 18c; 19a; 20c; 21d; 22d; 23a

Guide to Documents

I-1b; II-1c; III-1c

Significant Individuals

1a; 2e; 3d; 4r; 5j; 6f; 7c; 8p; 9b; 10n; 11q; 12h 13s; 14k; 15o; 16i; 17m; 18g; 19l

Identification

1j; 2l; 3f; 4i; 5n; 6a; 7o; 8e; 9b; 10m; 11g; 12c; 13h; 14d; 15k